# Moving Abroad

First published in 2009 by
Liberties Press
Guinness Enterprise Centre | Taylor's Lane | Dublin 8
Tel: +353 (1) 415 1224
www.LibertiesPress.com | info@libertiespress.com

Distributed in the United States by
Dufour Editions | PO Box 7 | Chester Springs | Pennsylvania | 19425

and in Australia by
James Bennett Pty Limited | InBooks | 3 Narabang Way
Belrose NSW 2085

Trade enquiries to CMD Booksource
55A Spruce Avenue | Stillorgan Industrial Park
Blackrock | County Dublin
Tel: +353 (1) 294 2560 | Fax: +353 (1) 294 2564

ISBN: 978–1–905483–75–4
2 4 6 8 10 9 7 5 3 1

A CIP record for this title is available from the British Library.

Cover design by Ros Murphy
Internal design by Liberties Press
Printed in Ireland by Colour Books

# Moving Abroad

## The Irish Guide to Working and
## Living Overseas

## Niall Foley

# Contents

# Introduction

From fifteen-year-old Cork girl Annie Moore, the first passenger registered in Ellis Island, to the Wild Geese of the 1980s, modern Irish history has been characterised by waves of emigration.

The prevailing tendency has always been to view those emigrating merely as victims of desperate economic times. And today, many commentators are predicting another mass exodus of Ireland's brightest and best in search of better times elsewhere, as jobs dry up and the dole queues lengthen.

Often left out of this picture is the positive, proactive sense of adventure that has always prompted Irish people to explore pastures new – whatever the situation at home. It is a spirit – perhaps engendered by being an island nation, surrounded by the call of the sea – that has seen the Irish make considerable political, social, economic and cultural contributions in countries across the globe. The warmth of the Irish is a cliché that retains its truth. If you have holidayed or travelled abroad, I'm sure you have at least one story of how a complete stranger wanted to do you a good turn, or a Customs guard dropped his 'bad cop' demeanour, when they identified you as Irish.

The Irish have made their mark all over the globe, and not just through the ubiquitous local Irish bar, either.

There are countless Irish individuals the world over who are living interesting lives and seizing enriching opportunities that may not have been proffered had they remained at home.

If you are reading this book, it is because you too are considering the opportunities that lie elsewhere.

Are you a grandparent hoping to start a fresh chapter of your life in pastures new? Or a single person who wants to fulfil a dream or follow a temptation? Perhaps you are a parent aiming to raise your children in a better place. Maybe you have recently finished college and beginning your career in Europe has long been on your mind – or maybe you are a worker who has suddenly been offered an intriguing role in Dubai.

Whatever category you fall into, and especially if it's none of the above, you'll appreciate that moving to another country is not a passive response to difficulties in Irish society, but rather a positive step towards seizing enriching opportunities elsewhere.

And whatever destination you choose, from Australia to Zanzibar, the same important questions need to be asked: What are the work prospects? What are the visa requirements? Is your current pension transferable? How do you go about buying or renting property? What about schools, health care, tax and general money matters – before and after your move?

When you consider the sheer number of basic nuts-and-bolts issues you'll need to factor in (and we haven't even mentioned pets, certificates of good character, or vaccinations yet), your relaxing dream of a new life abroad may turn into a logistical nightmare of headache-inducing proportions.

And you're right to be aware of the traps that may at worst halt, and at best hinder, your potential move. Along with a death in the family and serious personal injury, moving home is considered one of the major traumatic events in one's life.

In 2000, I made the relatively short relocation to Dublin from London. As I was in my early twenties, single, and had no significant financial commitments, you would think that the move would have been simply a case of packing the suitcase and going. But even such a seeminly straightforward move became complicated in time, thanks to my 'it'll be grand' attitude.

Firstly, I made the mistake of packing sentimentally. I brought my favourite books, LPs and CDs – and forgot job references, A-Level certificates and other astoundingly obvious documents.

Additionally, I didn't wrap up my tax affairs cleanly, and so Her Majesty's Inland Revenue – who suspected me of being a major tax evader – haunted me with letters. Things were complicated further when I went back to London to work for a summer. After much correspondence, I finally cut through the Inland Revenue's bureaucracy and spoke to a real-life human being with an actual name. They were incredibly professional, polite, and helpful. But because I hadn't tidied up my affairs correctly, I fell into the endless red tape of the system. It took much more effort and time to emerge than if I had taken just a little care in the first place.

It would have been well worth the phone call, too – in the end, it worked out that they owed *me* a tax rebate of several hundred pounds, and not the other way round.

The lesson is that whatever the move, whether great or small, the same pieces of the jigsaw have to be carefully put in place in order to guarantee a stress-free life abroad – and to ensure ease of return if things don't work out.

When you bear in mind the added dimension of wrapping up your affairs in Ireland before leaving to live and work in a new culture, as well as planning your new life abroad, the task at hand may seem overwhelming.

However, like many of life's seemingly gigantic difficulties, the daunting prospect of moving and working abroad can be a hassle-free experience with the aid of clear guidelines and sensible, diligent planning.

I'm writing this book in the hope that it will enable you to open the gateway to the rest of your life.


The last few years has witnessed a substantial increase in the number of us emigrating. The Central Statistics Office estimates that 45,300 people left Ireland in 2008 in order to live abroad. This is up from 42,000 in 2007 and 36,000 in 2006. In fact, the 2008 figure for emigration from Ireland is the highest since 1991.

This increase isn't explained by Ireland's Celtic Tiger years, when it seemed that status anxiety demanded that everyone have an overseas property portfolio, and, conversely, neither is it explained by the subsequent downturn.

A major factor in the rise has been the freedom of Irish people to move to another European Union country through the expansion of the EU (Cyprus, the Czech Republic, Estonia, Hungary, Latvia, Lithuania, Malta, Poland, Slovakia and Slovenia all joined the EU in 2004, while Bulgaria and Romania joined in 2007).

Elsewhere, the governments of Australia, New Zealand and Canada have sought to boost economic growth by filling their skills shortages through immigration, and have increased the number of visas they grant each year accordingly.

While tighter security measures and visa regulations since 9/11 means that America is not the go-to destination for Irish people that it once was, the States retains a special mythology for Irish emigrants. While visa opportunities are limited, the US government does recognise the potential economic contribution of skilled immigrants.

And when you take into account a highly competitive aviation industry, which means that it is as cheap to fly either long or short haul as it has ever been, then clearly, the Irish have more scope to move abroad than they have ever enjoyed before.

For these reasons, most people know a friend, or a friend of a friend, who has moved abroad in recent years. And human nature being what it is, it's all too easy to feel jealous when imagining the lives of those who have moved to somewhere with a warmer climate and a cheaper cost of living . . . maybe cycling to work along the seafront with a fresh pastry in the basket, the cute hoors.

However, the grass isn't always greener, and we tend not to imagine the stressful and nerve-racking process they went through, or the tricky settling-in period, or even the depression of a sweet dream turned sour.

## The migration business

Moving costs money, and there are many companies and individuals who will offer their professional services. Unfortunately, the lack of a comprehensive regulatory framework means that inevitably, some shoddy operators are out there.

And as moving abroad involves a broad range of tasks, from the practicalities of transporting and trans-ferring money to plotting a course through the often-muddy waters of immigration bureaucracy, the potential emigrant faces many potential dangers. The risk factors are heightened when you have to negotiate unfamiliar rules and regulations in an unfamiliar language.

And while the amount of well-intentioned first-hand information on moving abroad available through blogs and forums has never been greater, dependable and independent sources of information may be hard to find.

Thus, moving abroad may suddenly be appearing to be a far riskier venture than you may have imagined. And if you go about the move in a spirit of naive excitement or even, dare I say it, with an Irish 'sure, it'll be grand' attitude, you could well be setting yourself up for a demoralising – and very costly – fall.

## Make the *right* move

Whichever way you look at it, moving abroad is going to cost money, time and emotion, for you as well as your partner and family, if they are moving too. The investment will be well spent if you begin the process with the right steps, and will help you realise your dream of starting a fulfilling new life abroad.

But get it wrong and you will either have an unhappy experience abroad or make an unscheduled and, ultimately, possibly embarrassing return to Ireland. It'll be a lot easier to live with if you can blame bad luck. But if you lose out on your dream because of bad planning and bad judgement, the cloud could linger over your life in Ireland for years.

## Are you ready to emigrate?

With clear, sensible and logical planning, your daydream of a life abroad can become your everyday reality. But it is important to realise at an early stage of the emigration process that there will be some testing and challenging times ahead. Now is the time to ask yourself if you and your family members will *really* be able to cope with the move and make a new life abroad?

Throughout the book, there will be times to pause and reflect on the process. Take a moment now to gauge how ready you are to emigrate, and how you're likely to feel in the weeks and months ahead. For example:

*How have you felt when moving and starting a job somewhere new?*

If you found it to be stressful and felt overburdened by responsibility, be realistic about how you will deal with the added burden of, for example, moving your belongings hundreds of miles while simultaneously arranging to sell your car, or starting in a job with new procedures and a new working culture.

*How easy do you find it to meet new people?*

If you are genuinely a mixer, you'll quickly make a network of new friends and colleagues. But if you find meeting people and making friends difficult, your first few months may be spent online and on the telephone to friends you have left behind.

*How well have you coped when things went wrong on a holiday?*

Did you demonstrate the perseverance and stubbornness to get your point across, even when under pressure and despite language difficulties?

*How have you managed when you moved house?*

If you were driven mad by the movers or couldn't stand living out of boxes, imagine your frustration when you factor in the possibility of your possessions being delayed for a month, or your intended new home not being available until weeks later than planned.

*How important is your wider family and circle of friends, especially in times of crisis?*

Are you the type of person who is always there for friends or family when there's an emergency? Then bear in mind that when you get the call while you're abroad, you won't be able to rush there and be the shoulder to cry on. It may be days before you manage to get home – if you can manage it at all. Very early on, you'll have to accept that this is part and parcel of moving abroad, otherwise your new life will, quite literally, be a guilt trip.

Your new life will require commitment and a passion to enjoy the experience – tempered by clear thinking, and the determination to overcome the challenges that will inevitably come your way.

# 1

# Deciding to Make the Move

## First steps

You may well have your ideal destination in mind and, quite probably, the vivid image of your new life abroad has often caressed you to sleep on dreary Sunday nights or got you through dull Wednesday-morning coffee breaks.

But to get there, you will have to make a series of potentially life-changing decisions, not least of which is: just where is the best 'there' for you?

And way before you think about packing and booking flights, you'll need a critical assessment of your aims and ambitions. This way, you can lay solid foundations for what may be the most significant financial and emotional hurdles that will ever face you and your family.

Though there are a variety of reasons to consider moving abroad, they can broadly be divided into four groups: family, work, cost of living, and lifestyle. If you are to fulfil your emigration potential, you and any family members also making the move must understand the 'push' and 'pull' factors motivating your move, and how you can realistically manage such a major change.

Firstly, when considering your reasons for emigrating, start with a list of objectives and put them in order of priority. Consider these prompts:

## Family matters

Are you hoping to live somewhere safer for you and your family?

Do you want to move closer to friends or relatives living abroad?

Do you aim to have a better work/life balance?

Do you want a better education for your children, with more exposure to different languages?

## Work

Do you have career aspirations that cannot be fulfilled in Ireland or that you want to pursue elsewhere?

Are you qualified in a profession (such as a teacher or nurse) that is in higher demand in other countries?

Are you mulling over an attractive job offer abroad?

What wage expectations have you?

How many hours are you willing to work?

What level of job satisfaction do you hope to achieve?

How far will you be willing to commute?

What holiday entitlement do you expect?

## Cost of living

Do you want to move somewhere with a cheaper cost of living and lower tax rates?

Do you want to own a bigger property?

What type of property are you hoping for?

What is your budget? (Be realistic!)

What location do you have in mind? Do you see yourself living in the city, in a business district, in the country, or by the sea?

How big a mortgage are you willing to take on?

What percentage of your salary do you want as disposable income?

## Lifestyle

Do you aim to live somewhere with a more relaxed lifestyle? What pace of life do you want?

Do you want to escape the Irish weather and live in sunnier, warmer climes? Or do you want to live in colder, snowier countries where you can enjoy winter sports all year round?

Did you enjoy your holiday somewhere so much that you want to live there?

Do you enjoy a hobby or sport that you can develop further abroad?

What recreational activities do you want you or your family to access while abroad?

Are there any specific attractions you want to be near?

Do you want to be close to beaches and parks?

Is it important to be part of an Irish community? (Or to have easy access to Guinness, Taytos and GAA coverage when you need some home comforts?)

To reflect on why you want to emigrate, take some time with a cup of tea to write a list of your emigration goals. They can draw on the above points, or other reasons that haven't been mentioned. The list will prove useful when contemplating which country to move to, why you want to move, and exactly what you're looking for. And reflect critically on your own personal qualities and resolve: have you got what it takes to make a successful move?

## Involving your Family

If you're planning to move abroad alone, you should still involve your family, if only because they may be able to offer support. When to tell your parents, grandparents and siblings that you plan to move away from Ireland is a big decision, but hopefully, the earlier you tell them, the greater opportunity they will have to support your decision.

Moreover, if you are moving with family (a partner, children, or both), they will need to be involved in the decision. Even if better career prospects make it seem as though moving is an open-and-shut case, it is likely to be the biggest single decision the family will ever make together, and so everyone should feel they are included.

On the other hand, you don't want to rush into announcing the project to your family before you have explored whether there are any restrictions which will see your visa application turned down.

If the plan is for your partner to join you, they should make a list of emigration motivations too – without having looked at yours first! Hopefully, a shared pattern of ambitions will emerge. If not, you may have to compromise on the points where your ideals clash.

You also need to think about how your children will adapt. Consider:

Will the move make them happier?

Should you take them away from their home to follow *your* dreams?

Do you have *their* best interests at heart, or your own?

How much can (and should) you involve them in the emigration process?

The age of your children will ultimately determine how much they are involved in the project. If they are very young, they probably won't have a full grasp of the changes involved. On the other hand, persuading a teenager to move in those oh-so-difficult years may prove difficult.

But either way, encouraging your children to join in the process as early as possible is a positive step. If they do their own research and set their own aims and motivations, the benefits of the move may suddenly become clear to them; whether it's making new friends, playing new sports, or even driving at a much younger age than is possible in Ireland. (In New Zealand and parts of Canada, for instance, the minimum driving age is fifteen, whereas in some American states people as young as fourteen can get behind the wheel!) However, Irish youths may be dismayed to learn that the alcohol age restriction of twenty-one is enforced rigorously across the US – except in dry cities, where alcohol sales are prohibited to young people and adults alike.

Of course, for many Irish people who are considering living and working abroad, family concerns are their main reason for moving. You may want to broaden the experiences of your children, increase the opportunities open to them, or secure a better standard of living for the entire family by living in a culture with a more enjoyable work/life balance.

## Safety

Given the continuing spate of gangland shootings reported in the media, one could be forgiven for thinking that Ireland's cities are spiralling are out of control. In reality, the inner cities of Dublin and Limerick are a long way from being the drug-scarred environments they were in the 1980s, while the ongoing peace process in Northern Ireland has seen political violence stabilised to a greater degree than would have been predicted even a decade ago.

Despite this, the anecdotal perception is that crime in Ireland is rising relentlessly, with everyday experiences of anti-social behaviour becoming more and more prevalent. Unquestionably, some people moving from Ireland are doing so to secure a safer existence for their family.

But crime exists all over the world, and your choice of location within a given country will play a large part in determining the risks that your family are likely to face. Moving to a sedate, rural area, however, may deprive your family of the employment, education and cultural opportunities available in urban areas – which generally have higher crime rates.

## Work/life balance

There is a particular postcard that tourists to Ireland seem to love. It says 'Rush hour, Ireland' and has a picture of a cow standing alone in the main street of a non-descript town.

Believe it or not, there are people in the world who receive these postcards and think that they are an accurate representation of Irish life.

And if you think it's just gullible Yanks who are taken in by that type of blarney nonsense, you're wrong. Not long after moving to Ireland, I visited my parents in their small town in the west. I made the passing remark to a local woman that I liked the sleepy, relaxed pace of life there. She took affront and set me straight. 'It's not a sleepy town at all,' she said. 'Far from it.' She was right. Before my eyes were people getting up at the crack of dawn to drop the kids to the crèche, commuting massive distances to work, putting in long hours, and coming home to farm duties in the evening, not to mention all the usual domestic and family chores.

I was living at a slower, 'holiday' pace, and took it for granted that everyone else was, too. So if the aim of an improved work/life balance is the main reason for your move, make sure you don't make the easy mistake that being on holiday somewhere and working and living there will provide the same, or even a similar, experience.

Also, be wary of national stereotypes, such as imagining that life in Spain will consist of short working days and hot lazy afternoon siestas, or that if you don't find work in France, you can always shack up with an artist in a garret by the Seine and spend the rest of your life talking about the meaning of life and why you hate Americans.

With jobs here scarce, and increasing competition for the vacancies that do arise, Irish working culture has changed. Greater insecurity is fuelling longer hours and placing greater demands on workers. The recession is affecting many places in the world, however, so be wary of thinking it will be different elsewhere.

Bear in mind too that, even if you feel confident that your move will result in an improved work/life balance in the long term, every spare minute of the first few months of your new life will be taken up with countless things to do.

## Work aspirations

While redressing their work/life balance may be the inspiration for many, others move abroad to further their career, or because they have had a job offer. There is an abundance of qualified teachers and health care professionals in Ireland, while employment in the public service sector has fallen off considerably. For such professionals, moving to countries that are crying out for their skills is an option worth considering.

You may find, however, that working in the local labour force requires high-level language skills. If you limit yourself to English-speaking services within foreign countries, you will have a very limited scope indeed. Do you have foreign language skills, or the determination to put in the work needed to ramp up your knowledge successfully?

The alternative is being one of those people (you know the ones I mean: the English you meet in Spain) who live for years in a country and remain ignorant of the language.

Even if English is widely used, being prepared to learn the official language will open many cultural opportunities that would otherwise remain inaccessible to you. After coming to Ireland, I began studying the Irish language. Even a basic understanding of the language has given me cherished insights into Irish life I would not otherwise have had.

## Cost of living

The summer of 2009 saw the annual rate of deflation in Ireland rise to 4.7 percent, a level not seen since 1933. And as a result of lower prices and falling rents, an international cost of living survey published by Mercer in July 2009 ranks Dublin as the twenty-fifth most expensive of 143 cities, a drop of nine places since 2008.

Despite this, Ireland remains a comparatively expensive place to live. For example, a cup of coffee in Dublin costs €3 on average, which is more than in London, Rome, Amsterdam, Madrid or Vancouver. And while such surveys are always open to argument – and fluctuating exchange rates – it can be broadly stated that you are likely to encounter lower prices when you move away from Ireland. Correspondingly, you may also earn a lower wage, but find that your money goes further.

To get a comprehensive picture, you'll need to look at the wages you can expect to get in your destination of choice, then take into account national and local taxes, potential mortgage repayments, utility costs, medical insurance, car insurance, school fees, and the cost of fuel and groceries. Free and paid-for international salary comparison information is available from websites such as *www.payscale.com* and *www.salaryexpert.com*. And don't forget to research local charges that do not apply in Ireland, such as water rates and community poll tax.

Needless to say, even with the most realistic planning, it's human nature to underestimate how much you'll need. Emigrants often find that money doesn't go as far as they had hoped. But with thorough research and a bit of budget planning, you can prepare your finances for the realities of emigration.

## Lifestyle and leisure

Many people move abroad to pursue hobbies and pastimes in more suitable climates. Skiers, for example, may find themselves gravitating towards the French, Swiss or Italian Alps.

But lifestyle and leisure activities are not enjoyed by osmosis. For years, I lived besides the Oval cricket ground in London but never stepped inside it. Make a balanced decision by asking yourself how seriously you intend to pursue the particular interests, and whether they are important enough to you (and your family) to warrant the significant upheaval that will be involved.

## Climate

When we go on holiday in the summer months, we often see the best of our ideal destination. Later, back in the cold grey reality of an Irish autumn, our thoughts drift back to the summer break, basking in the eternal sunshine of our memories.

But of course, the weather changes throughout the year in your holiday destination, too. So if climate is a big factor in your reasoning, do some thorough research on year-round temperatures and conditions before beginning the emigration process. Ideally, actual exposure to seasonal temperatures in your chosen destination will help prevent you from making a costly mistake. A good source of basic climate data is the BBC weather website, *www.bbc.co.uk/weather*.

# Pitfalls to avoid

Although there are often common themes shared by people who are considering a move abroad, an individual's decision to move to pastures new will always be made in unique circumstances. And while there are no easy, scientific approaches to pinpointing the right location, there are some obvious (but oh-so-tempting) pitfalls to avoid.

### 'We had a great holiday'
When you're having a great time on holiday somewhere, it's entirely natural to daydream about what it would be like to live there.

But what makes holidays so special is, of course, that they are a break from the humdrum routine of our everyday life, so don't be misled by your holiday bubble:

> Your time is your own on holiday, unlike the confines of your weekly routine. But if you move abroad, will you really have the time to pursue the leisure activities you enjoy on holiday, especially in those hectic initial months?

> You tend to spend more on holiday than you do at home.

> Prices may seem cheaper – but look at prices from the perspective of local wages rather than your Irish salary.

### 'It looked great on film'
Without question, some people take inspiration from films and television programmes they have seen,

whether it is a beautiful movie such as *The Darjeeling Limited* or an interesting TV travel series hosted by Michael Palin. And while the inspiration may prove invaluable in launching your research, don't plan your life according to fantasy.

## 'Someone I know emigrated there'

If you know someone who has moved abroad, it can motivate you towards making a similar choice, especially if they are a close friend or family member; they may seem to offer a ready-made support network for your move.

Bear in mind, however, that even the most honest people often try to put on their best face, especially when reporting on something they have invested a lot of time and emotion in. So while you may get glowing reports of golden sunsets, your friend may not be telling you about the eccentricities of local plumbing or their panic about failing to land a job as quickly as they had hoped. There's no substitute for making your own fact-finding trip.

## Because we can move there

While all Irish citizens can move freely through the EU, some others may be eligible for visas and permits to live in Australia, New Zealand, Canada or the United States.

But just because you *can* move somewhere, it doesn't necessarily mean that you *should*. Your destination should be somewhere you really want to move to, and if you find you can't get a visa for a specific destination, think carefully before uprooting yourself and your family just for the sake of moving somewhere else.

# Have you got what it takes?

## Essential attributes

As well as an understanding of the emigration process, you must be able to anticipate and manage your own frame of mind and attitude, as well as those of the people around you. There are some important personal qualities you will need to call upon. These include:

Commitment and determination in achieving your goals

The ability to manage change

The flexibility required to succeed at trouble-shooting and problem-solving

A positive yet realistic outlook on life.

Although you can anticipate most problems in the emigration process, there will be some unexpected curveballs coming your way. The immigration process entails a series of challenges that begins long before you step on a plane and continues long after you get the key to your new home. But even accepting that these challenges are coming your way will help you to deal with them – including the unexpected ones – more effectively.

## What next?

Having thought about why you should go and what inner strengths you will need to make the move succeed, it's time to pinpoint where in the world to launch your new life.

# 2

# Choosing the Right Country for You

## Can you emigrate?

### The immigration maze

Unless you're one of a fortunate few who aren't burdened by such concerns, you'll be planning to work abroad. Your choice of destination then will be determined by where you can find work and whether the immigration department will grant you a visa.

If you are planning to emigrate with children, the time it takes to obtain authorised paperwork in your preferred destinations will help make up your mind which is the one for you.

Indeed, negotiating the visa maze is perhaps the most perplexing aspect of the moving process. Whichever destination you favour, there will be officialese to comprehend and bureaucratic frustrations to endure.

For EU member countries, the most important document to have is an up-to-date Irish passport. But each country has its own rules and regulations, and you may be frustrated in obtaining permanent residence paperwork, particularly where English is not widely spoken and your language skills are limited.

Applicants may find that in some countries, such as Australia, New Zealand, Canada and the US, getting the visa paperwork to update their passports can be a

prolonged process, whereas it is then much easier to obtain subsequent paperwork. You do have the option, of
course, of hiring professional help to guide you through
the immigration maze, but it will be a significant added
cost to the burgeoning fees of processing visa and
residency/employment permits.

While European states may have the reputation of
drowning in red tape – France and Switzerland among
them – in fact Canada and America rank among the slow-
est when it comes to immigration procedures. For example, the wait for a Canadian Skilled Worker visa is around
forty-two to forty-eight months (see *www.canada.org.uk*
for more information), while the immigration sponsoring of siblings or adult children to America can take up
to seven years.

So as you can see, before your excitement and dreams
about any particular country start building, you need to
research the immigration maze for the destination you
have in mind in order to determine what chance you
have of being successful in your application.

## Work

Continuing your career after moving abroad will entail
the same challenges of finding a job as you would expect
in Ireland. However, some career qualities you have re-
lied on in the past may be lost in translation when you
move abroad.

While your skills and experience will remain vital, you
may have a problem in having your Irish qualifications
recognised. In addition, some professions, such as the
legal professions, may require a local licence.

Of course, you will need to know beforehand if your
skills and abilities are in demand in the country of your
choice, and your preferred location within that country.
You may feel tempted to say that you will do anything
(particularly if you have golden memories of a J1 visa

summer spent flipping burgers by day and necking beers by night), but such novelties soon become tiresome, and issues such as job satisfaction and salary do not become any less important when you leave Ireland.

Another element to take into consideration is that workers in Ireland are typically entitled to more holiday days than in some countries. Many American workers, for example, are entitled to only ten vacation days a year. Here are the average annual holiday entitlements for some of the most popular destinations for Irish emigrants:

| | |
|---|---|
| France | 30 days |
| United Kingdom | 24 days |
| Portugal | 22 days |
| Spain | 22 days |
| Cyprus | 20 days |
| Italy | 20 days |
| Germany | 20 days |
| Australia | 20 days |
| New Zealand | 20 days |
| Canada | 10 days |
| United States | 10 days |

## Working in the EU

A work permit is not required to work in the EU. Having said that, in all likelihood you will have to register your presence with the appropriate authorities and obtain official paperwork. For example, in Spain, you cannot be considered for a job unless you have a *número de identificación de extranjero* (NIE). Contrast this with France, where a *carte de séjour* is not technically necessary for finding work, and you'll see that each country, even under the umbrella heading of the EU, has its own immigration laws and cultures that must be respected.

The EURES network was established by the European Commission to help European citizens looking for work in another country in the EU/EEA. EURES has a network of advisers who can give you general practical information on legislation, social security, living conditions, useful addresses, information on pay levels, taxes, contracts, recruitment practices, and so on. They also have a database of vacancies in the EU/EEA. If you are interested in working in the EU/EEA, make an appointment with your nearest EURES advisor. Contact your nearest FÁS office for more information.

Although on paper it is relatively easy to work in the EU, in practice there are stumbling blocks to finding employment. Firstly, you will be competing against native speakers whose qualifications will be more familiar to employers than, for example, the Leaving Certificate, or a Higher Diploma in Teaching. For further advice on getting your qualifications recognised abroad, contact the National Qualifications Authority of Ireland at *www.qualificationsrecognition.ie.*

Of course, if you have the language skills to 'translate' your qualifications so that they are readily comparable to those of native job applicants, you will have an added edge in the jobs market.

As well as looking for a job related to your field, there are four other employment possibilities you may be considering:

Working for industries that cater for English-speaking communities

Setting up your own business

Working remotely for an Irish firm

Commuting to Ireland from abroad.

Catering for English-speaking communities will mean living in an area with an established English-speaking population or one that is popular with British or Irish tourists. Much of the work will be seasonal, service-industry employment, such as hotels and bar work, while some tradespeople will also be in demand. But limiting your employment prospects to a narrow choice of destinations will obviously hamper the breadth of your experiences abroad, and is unlikely to be a good long-term option.

The lure of being your own boss is always attractive, whether at home or abroad, and so you may be considering shaping your career in an entrepreneurial direction. This is not a task to be taken lightly if you plan to move abroad and establish a business immediately. The typical start-up difficulties you would expect in Ireland are exacerbated abroad when you take into consideration the added problems of unfamiliar tax laws and language issues.

If you have the possibility of working remotely for your Irish employer, make a realistic appraisal of your job security and look at the state of the job market locally, in case things don't work out. Pursuing this option means that you will be highly unlikely to fulfil the visa requirement for Australia, New Zealand, Canada or America. Whether or not you have a home in Ireland, and other factors, may affect your tax liability, and this is something that needs to be considered as well.

Working remotely in Europe for a few days and commuting to the Irish office once a week may be economically viable, thanks to the low-cost airline industry. While flying times may give you the impression that Ireland is only a couple of hours away from mainland Europe, bear in mind that low-cost airlines tend to use regional airports, which are sometimes hours from the city you need to get to. Take into account the time spent going through airports and the inevitable delays, and you'll have a more realistic picture of your commute. Don't rely on just one service operator, either. In the volatile and ultra-competitive world of aviation, airlines are continually scrutinising the cost-effectiveness of their routes and making changes, sometimes withdrawing services completely.

## Working outside the EU

You have to be something special to work in Australia, New Zealand, America or Canada. In fact, to qualify for a visa, your employer may have to prove that that no suitably qualified native citizen is available to take the job.

Needless to say, this makes things difficult. It is hard to imagine that there are many areas of specialisation that someone from the Irish workforce can offer to the job market in America, a global superpower with a population of just under 307 million.

Indeed, the American immigration department's list of skills that are in demand is very short. But some applications are accepted: a friend of mine enjoyed two years working as a stonemason on a skilled-employment visa.

Australia, New Zealand and Canada are certainly more proactive in their recruitment of foreign nationals, and publish a much broader list of skills and professions that their economies are in need of than the US immigration authorities. If you are a health care professional, for example, you might be interested to know that your skills are highly sought after.

The Australian economy is steady, with 1,200 new jobs having been added to the market in January 2009, while New Zealand currently has a strong demand for primary school teachers.

Canada, meanwhile, is experiencing its lowest unemployment rate in thirty years and unprecedented economic growth. As labour shortages increase, the Canadian government has introduced numerous migration programmes to find skilled migrants to fill vacancies from entry-level to senior positions. Between 129,300 and 144,600 visas have been made available for 2009.

The typical qualifications procedure to obtain a skilled-employment visa is via a points-test, with scores awarded for education, experience, and so on. Other personal details, such as character, health, and whether you have a criminal record, will also play a part in the evaluation process. But even if you seem to fulfil all the necessary requirements, things may still not be simple. Consider the following:

JOB TITLES While the job title may be identical to the one used in Ireland, there could be a variation in the duties expected of you. Again, the onus is on you to take steps in researching whether the duties and qualifications expected of someone in your position overseas corresponds to your job description in Ireland.

EXAMS You may have to sit an exam to continue working in your field in your new home country. Health care and law are two of the professions that are often licensed by local trade bodies.

QUALIFICATIONS Education and training frameworks differ from country to country. It may be essential for you to have your qualifications assessed and validated by the relevant organisation, such as Australia's Trades Recognition Authority, the New Zealand Qualifications Authority, or one of Canada's Foreign Credential Referral Offices. I did something similar when I had my A-Level results assessed in terms of Leaving Cert points for a college application.

Emigrating will require you to strike an appropriate balance between economic and lifestyle considerations. On the one hand, you may want to 'get away from it all', but find that this desire is compromised by the necessity of living in an urban or industrialised area where more jobs are available and your skills are needed.

Some visa opportunities, such as regional immigration schemes, make this dilemma redundant by requiring you to settle in the area in question. South Australia and British Columbia are two districts that operate regional visa schemes, whereby the offer of a visa is usually tied in with a specific job. (For information on regional support for migrants to South Australia, see *www.immigration.sa.gov.au*.)

If you do not go down the regional-visa route, a two-step approach may be useful in trying to find the right balance. If, in the short term, you go where the work is in the country of your choice, then, with a spell in the workforce under your belt, you can relocate to your preferred region later on.

Qualifying for a skilled-employment visa can be difficult, particularly with regards to American immigration, which demands a high level of education and experience in a particular occupation. If you are a newcomer to a profession or trade, you have almost no chance of making a successful case.

## Culture Shock

Depending on where you move, you may have to overcome language issues. But wherever you choose to live, you will be tested by cultural challenges, either big or small, on a daily basis.

The success of your emigration will be greatly determined by your ability to cope with culture-shock challenges, as well as how adaptable you are to the general way of life in your new home. There will inevitably be some uncomfortable or unsteady moments in the disorientating settling-in period.

Be prepared to commit completely to your cultural surroundings: it's the only way your project will be successful. And even when you feel like a fish out of water, try to avoid getting trapped into the pattern of continually making negative comparisons between your new life and life back in Ireland.

## Language and education

If you move somewhere where English is not the first language, it will significantly affect your life – and not just in terms of your chances of finding a job. Even if you have sufficient language skills to get by on a day-to-day basis, there will be times, such as dealing with police or hospital staff in an emergency, when you need to communicate directly and quickly.

Language difficulties add a further layer of complication if you are a parent emigrating with children. Most schools in the destination of your choice will teach students using the official language of that country. Younger children tend to adapt better than older ones, but being thrown in at the deep end can be a daunting experience, on top of all the other changes. Private lessons prior to moving will, if nothing else, offer some exposure to the new language, hopefully making the language immersion post-relocation less dramatic.

An option available in some major cities is to enrol your child in a private school where children can continue to be taught through English. In some ways, though, this is just an expensive delaying tactic. At some point, if your children are to continue to live and work overseas as they get older, they will need the language skills necessary to get the most out of their new home.

Try to be aware also of language differences *within* countries. While Castilian Spanish is the language of government and trade, it is just one of several regional languages spoken in Spain: others include Basque, Catalan and Galician. And in Canada, the province of Quebec is officially francophone. An awareness of the languages used in each region will be important when making education-related decisions for your children.

Obviously, if you are moving to an English-speaking country, the choices you will have to make for your children's education will not focus on language issues.

## Money and health matters

With the best will in the world, money rarely goes as far as planned. While housing and health care costs are the two big burdens, there are countless other demands on your money. The costs of moving to another country include:

Research, in the form of books, internet usage, international phone calls and attending exhibitions

Selling your house, and possibly not getting the asking price

Moving your possessions overseas

Moving your pets abroad

Tax on pensions and investments

Flights

Accommodation on arrival

Property rental

Car costs, whether buying or renting

Health insurance

A get-by fund in case of unemployment.

Those moving to countries outside the EU must also factor in visa fees (which could range from €100 to €10,000, depending on the type of application) and immigration assistance (typically between €1,000 and €5,000, also depending on the type of application).

## Taking your pets with you

It is important to check the requirements for the country you plan to move to. But generally speaking, the process of taking pets overseas can include vaccinations, microchip identification, blood tests and, in some cases, quarantine, potentially running up bills of thousands of euros.

## Health care

Easy access to good health care should be of primary importance to you, particularly if you or a loved one has poor health or if you have reached retirement age. Health care provision should play a major part in your decision on where to move abroad.

In Europe, the health care systems are on a par or better than the Irish system, not least because France and Germany, for example, spend more of their GDP on health care provision than Ireland does. However, services are not always free of charge.

It is essential that you research the national and regional rules surrounding health care. When planning your emigration budget, take into account any insurance payments you may have to make for you and you family.

## The European Health Insurance Card

If you are an EU/EEA national and are travelling or staying temporarily in another state of the European Economic Area (EEA) or Switzerland, you are entitled to receive medical care if you become ill or have an accident. You can apply for the European Health Insurance Card (EHIC) through the HSE. To obtain health care with the card, you can go to the nearest public-system doctor, public hospital, or other public treatment centre and present your card.

Public health care systems vary from country to country, and few pay the full cost of health care for holders of the card, so there may be some element of co-payment for the services you receive.

Currently, the EEA comprises the twenty-seven member states of the European Union, together with Iceland, Norway and Liechtenstein. Your European Health Insurance Card is valid for use throughout any of these countries, and in Switzerland. You can apply for a card at *www.ehic.ie.*

## Police certificates

Depending on your visa application, you may be asked for a police certificate that shows you are of good character. Some overseas banks and employers may also request this. To obtain a police certificate, apply in writing to the superintendent in charge of your local district. Currently, there is no fee for this service.

## Vaccinations

Whether it's a short trip for research purposes or for a longer stay as part of the relocation process, a visit to some countries will require vaccinations. Even though Hong Kong, for instance, is a modern city with a good health care system, those heading there will require jabs for typhoid (ten days before travel), hepatitis A (two weeks before), diphtheria (three months before), tuberculosis (three months before) and hepatitis B (two months before). Your doctor or travel-health specialist will be able to advise you as to which destinations require vaccinations.

# Lifestyle and environment

One of the reasons you may be considering moving abroad is simply to avail of a sunnier climate. But while lazing on the beach in a hot country is all well and good, have you thought about how you will fare working in high temperatures and humidity, or about the increased danger of skin cancer?

Similarly, if you're going somewhere with a cold climate year-round, how would you cope with routinely having to drive in snow and ice?

## Climate change

Don't skip this part, even if you have no interest in green issues, because climate change could have a material impact on your decision to move abroad. Some factors to consider:

Will water shortages lead to an increase in rates?

Will a higher incidence of flooding put your new home at risk?

Will rising sea levels damage the coastline in your preferred destination?

Will melting glaciers and less snow reduce opportunities to enjoy winter sports?

## Wildlife

St Patrick may have driven the snakes from Ireland years ago, but he never made it to Australia. So if your skin crawls at the thought of poisonous snakes and spiders being nearby, a move Down Under may not be for you.

Although this is a dramatic example, a move from Ireland will result in a change in the climate, ecosystem and wildlife. Will you – and your children (and pets) – feel safe and be comfortable in your new surroundings?

## Decision time

If you are having trouble deciding between two or more countries, a good old-fashioned list of pros and cons for each destination should help you clarify your thoughts.

If you are emigrating with others, encourage them to add to the list.

## What next?

At this stage, your decision-making process should have reached one of the following points:

You are clear on your ambitions and focused on which country you want to move to.

You have an idea of your motivations and have a few countries in mind.

You have an idea of your motivations but no idea which is the right country.

The list of pros and cons should help sort the likely from the unlikely. Then it's on to the research to sort the facts from the fantasy.

# 3

## The Rules of Research

At this stage, you should have in mind a shortlist of potential destinations. The next part of the process is to deepen your knowledge of these countries, so that you make the best possible choice for you.

## Determining boundaries

The important initial step now is to work out what your emigration goals are and what information you need to determine whether these goals can be met.

If you have visited or spent time in a country you are thinking of emigrating to, you may feel that you don't need to bother too much about the research. But such carelessness may cost you quite a bit of money and heartbreak in the long run. If there are any surprises to be had, you want to discover them now. You're facing a decision that will mark a major change for you and your family and, to do yourself justice, you will need to undertake further research to build upon the information you have at this stage.

You might find some of the research boring, particularly when it comes to immigration rules and visa procedures. This is all vital information, though, so try to think of the bigger picture and the passion that is driving you to seek a new life abroad in the first place.

## Preliminary research

The amount of time and effort required here depends on how much you can be sure you know about your preferred destinations. A few evenings searching online might be enough, but if you need information from official sources, you might be kept waiting a week or two for a reply.

## Researching regulations

The first thing to ascertain before all else is simply whether you are eligible for a visa. Immigration regulations become more complex once you look beyond the EU. While you can conduct the research yourself, a shortcut is to recruit an immigration specialist. Irish immigration specialists (such as *www.anewlifeabroad.ie* and *www.visafirst.com*) offer a consultancy service, with some initial services – such as whether you match skill sets required by immigration departments – free of charge.

## What do I need to find out?

With any research project, there is a danger that the boundaries are limitless. But there comes a point when a little less conversation and a little more action is required. To avoid a quagmire of endless procrastination, focus on identifying your goals, and determining whether they are realistic. And while this somewhat functional information is absolutely necessary, you should also seek out personal experience and first-hand accounts to add to the impressions you have gathered. Your research categories could look like this:

CLIMATE

LIFESTYLE, LEISURE AND CULTURE

PEOPLE AND ATTITUDES

HEALTH AND WELL-BEING

EMPLOYMENT

EDUCATION

CHILDHOOD

FINANCIAL MATTERS

LANGUAGE

IMMIGRATION

TRANSIT TIME

FEARS

With IMMIGRATION, for example, you could record you goals like this:

EMIGRATION GOAL: To move to a country where my skills and profession are in demand, offering good chances of a successful visa application.

RESEARCH GOAL: To identify if there are any regional visas within the country under consideration that would offer such an opportunity.

INFORMATION REQUIRED: Details of immigration regulations, the visa application process, visa charges, waiting times, and the ratio of visas on offer to actual applications.

Another good rule of research is to keep a tidy filing system, otherwise it will get very messy, and digging out information you have already found will be as big a pain as finding it in the first place.

## Sources of information

Immigration and health care systems can change fre-quently, so bear in mind that while information on emigration is available from a wide range of sources, not all of it will be up to date and relevant.

## Where to find information

OFFICIAL SOURCES, such as government and statistical websites

UNOFFICIAL SOURCES, including printed-media and property websites. Just remember that they may be offering only a partial view. It is the company's job to persuade you to invest in one way or another in a given location, and your job to look for data that contradicts what they say or to propose equally suitable alternatives.

FIRST-HAND EXPERIENCE, whether on a holiday or business trip

SECOND-HAND INFORMATION. This includes experiences related by family and friends.

# Internet

## Government immigration websites

If you have an EU destination in mind, the best port of call will be the country's official embassy or consulate in Ireland. The French Embassy in Dublin, for instance, has a wealth of visa information on its website, *www.ambafrance.ie.*

While the embassies of Australia, New Zealand, Canada and America will also be able to provide visa information, the immigration department of each administration has useful websites outlining the requirement for each visa class of category, a self-assessment tool for the most popular skills-based visas, downloadable application forms, and a range of introductory information about the location, climate, people, employment opportunities, relocation process and various regions. Here are some of the main immigration websites:

| | |
|---|---|
| America | *www.uscis.gov* |
| Australia | *www.immi.gov.au* |
| Canada | *www.cic.ga.ca* |
| Europe | *www.euimmigration.org* |
| New Zealand | *www.immigration.govt.nz* |

## Online forums and social networking

The huge range of discussion boards and social networking sites online can be a very useful resource for getting people's general impressions and help with specific queries. Some people who emigrate also blog about their experiences, meaning that you can pick up some good tips – and hopefully learn from their mistakes!

Remember, though, that not all the accounts you read will be comprehensive, nor are your queries likely to be answered by an expert. Also, ask yourself who is running the website: a property agent or other figure with a vested interest may be behind it. Double-check any important information with other sources.

## Weather

Whereas Met Éireann only provides information on Ireland, the UK government metrological office (available at *www.metoffice.gov.uk*) offers weather information, past and present, on every region in the world. Details available include average temperatures, sunshine, rainfall and daylight hours year-round.

## Country profiles

The Organisation for Economic Co-operation and Development (*www.oecd.org*) offers a breakdown of national statistics for individual countries, including facts about population, economy and employment.

Many European governments also have web resources offering important data on their societies, including Spain's National Statistical Institute (*www.ine.es*), France's National Institute for Statistics and Economics Studies (*www.insee.fr*) and Italy's National Statistical Institute (*www.istat.it*). The websites, Deutschland Portal (*www.deutschland.de*), Facts about Germany (*www.tasachen-ueber-deutschland.de*) and the federal government website (*www.bundesregierung.de*) give a range of information on Germany and the government's policies.

## Flights

Websites such as *www.ebookers.ie* and *www.skyscanner.net* will help you to gauge the choice and frequency of air services to your intended destination, by simultaneously searching many airline schedules. This information could prove to be invaluable when calculating the cost of travelling back to Ireland from abroad, as well as working out how quickly, and at what cost, Irish friends and family can visit you.

## Schools

Lists of schools can be found on the department of education website, and local government pages, of your preferred destination.

## Involving your children

Getting your children involved in the research process can boost their interest in the overall project. Whether this is by looking for schools, researching potential new hobbies or learning about the local wildlife, they will start to see the personal benefits of the move and feel that they have a stake in the overall project.

## Economics and employment

There are numerous helpful websites which offer broad overviews on the economy and employment sectors of countries across the globe. For example, the *Economist*'s website (*www.economist.com/countries*) contains 'country briefings' which can offer statistics and an economic profile of where you intend to live and work.

America's Central Intelligence Agency has an interesting and free-to-browse World Factbook page (*www.cia.gov/library/publications/the-world-factbook/-index.html*), which provides information on the history, people, government, economy, geography, communications, transportation, military, and transnational issues for 266 world entities. The economy section provides a breakdown of labour forces by occupation, which is a useful tool for making a broad evaluation of whether your skills are in demand.

If you are planning a move to Canada, *www.working-incanada.gc.ca* is a great tool as it enables you to find information about wages and employment in specific areas.

For New Zealand, *www.immigration.govt.nz* provides a similar level of detail.

For research into the European labour market, visit *www.europa.eu*, where you can download the 'Europe in Figures' guide, which provides an up-to-date cost-of-living analysis.

Each year, Mercer compares fifty cities worldwide in a cost-of-living analysis. The useful overview is available for free at *www.mercerhr.com*.

And as you would when looking for a job in Ireland, a search through the websites of international job boards and recruiters will give you an indication of how likely you are to gain suitable employment in your preferred destination. Websites such as *www.escape-artist.com* features jobs by category and country, while *www.quintcareers.com* will refer you to employment agency links in the destinations you select. Additionally, you may find websites listing jobs internationally by profession or trade, such as *www.jobspublichealth.com* for public health jobs or *www.infooil.com* for jobs in oil and gas industries.

## Property

If you are thinking of buying a property overseas, the best source for reliable figures is the real-estate associations in the countries in question.

## Exhibitions

A good place to gather a range of information in one place is by attending an emigration exhibition. Although you should go expecting the 'hard sell' and being prepared to resist any pressure to jump into a commitment there and then, exhibitions may also present the opportunity to speak directly to government immigration departments, visa lawyers, removal companies, employers, and property and relocation service providers.

# Fact-finding trips

A fact-finding trip is the complete opposite of the 'sure, it'll be grand' approach. Rather than leaving your emigration in the hands of fate, such a trip could prove essential in helping you make up your mind. A fact-finding trip should focus on clear objectives and information you need to find out, and be treated as a serious endeavour, not as a holiday by another name.

Such a trip, especially to countries that are outside Europe or are not serviced by low-fare airlines, might seem like an unnecessary expense, but it could be very worthwhile if it clarifies in your mind whether a preferred destination really is or isn't for you.

## Seeking assistance

Relocation agents in America, Canada, Australia and New Zealand should be able to assist with the following:

Picking you up at the airport on arrival

Planning an itinerary

Hiring a car

Arranging furnished, short-term rental accommodation

General advice on what to research while you're in the area

The agent may also be able to guide you around various properties for sale or rent, to give you an idea of how much bang you can get for your buck. Do your best to ascertain that this is independent advice, and not just the agent promoting one particular developer or agency. *www.moving2australia.com* is a dedicated site aiming to assist with relocation to Australia, with *www.moving-2america.com* providing relocation services for America.

## Organising a fact-finding trip

Six key questions to ask are:

WHO SHOULD GO? Depending on how much time and money you can afford, ideally everyone who is emigrating should go on the trip.

WHEN SHOULD YOU GO? Obviously work and school conditions may dictate this to a degree, but it would be interesting to visit your preferred destination at different times of the year, for example during the main holiday season, and outside this season.

WHERE SHOULD YOU GO? This depends on your list of possibilities and how many places you can get to.

HOW LONG SHOULD YOU GO FOR? Be sure to give yourself more time in each destination than you think you will need. If you are planning a trip to a couple of destinations outside the EU, it may prove more cost-effective to take a longer trip and make the short haul between destinations, rather than paying for a number of international flights.

WHAT SHOULD YOUR OBJECTIVES BE? Your precise objectives will depend on whether you are, for instance, deciding between countries, or choosing between locations within a country. Check out the job scene, the culture, the weather – and if life there seems to be as good in reality as you dreamed.

HOW MUCH WILL IT COST? When you know where you are going and how long for, you can budget for the cost of flights, car hire and fuel, accommodation, travel insurance, food, and so on.

Finally, don't forget to make detailed notes and bring cameras and a video camera if you can get your hands on one. It's amazing how quickly details can be forgotten, especially when you have so much to take in.

## Fact-finding trips — Questions to ask yourself

What are my chances of getting a job I'd be happy with?

What would my new working routine be?

Where do my family and I want to live?

Is the cost of living high or low?

If you are emigrating with children, do the local schools have a good reputation? How much does an education cost?

What do Irish people living locally think of the area?

What is your feel for the local people?
What is the climate like?

## What next?

Once you have finished gathering information on a particular destination, the next step is to asses the data.

Remember your list of pros and cons from the last chapter? Now you have substantial evidence when it comes to evaluating each consideration.

If you plan to emigrate with members of your family, remember to include them in the assessment exercise.

And even if you are moving on your own, analyse your findings with trusted friends and relatives. Talk over your research with people you can rely on to give you an honest and constructive response.

Now you have a good understanding of one or more destinations that may be suitable for you, you may feel confident enough to continue the emigration process on your own. However, you may still consider availing of professional help with aspects of the process.

# 4

# Getting the Best Help

## Finding a professional

How much of the emigration process you can manage yourself depends on your confidence in researching important information, doing paperwork, dealing with bureaucracy, and organising your affairs. And depending on the country you want to move to, it may be worth considering hiring professional help.

In general, most people will find that moving to another country in the European Union is manageable. The endeavour, from completing the immigration paperwork to moving your possessions, is a series of tasks you should be able to organise successfully, perhaps by hiring local services if there are specific areas of difficulty.

The emigration process is far more complicated when you are moving out of the European Union, however. From immigration paperwork, to finding accommodation, to moving your possessions, there are professional services you can avail of, both here in Ireland and in your destination country, that are in a position to help. However, as with any service, there are a number of checks you should consider when making a choice.

CHECK CREDENTIALS Visit the website of the trade association or society endorsing the company in question.

ASK THE RIGHT QUESTIONS  Find out how much experience the company has in dealing with people in your situation, such as the specific type of visa you are applying for. If you are dealing with an overseas company and there is a language barrier, contact someone you can trust to translate for you, or, if necessary, hire an independent translator.

COMPARE COSTS  As you would with any service, get a few quotes from similar service providers, and if a fee is significantly higher or lower than for its competitors, try to find out why.

LOOK AT THE TIMING  Your preferred company may have many clients in peak seasons. If you plan to move at their busiest time of year, will this have an impact on the speed of service?

SEEK RECOMMENDATIONS  Industry awards and professional trade awards, as well as opinions sought through your network of friends and family, or via an internet forum, can be valuable in directing you to a reputable company.

## Relocations and removals

Moving home can be an exhausting and stressful exercise at the best of times. Factor in the cost and added stress of shipping possessions overseas and all the paperwork this entails, and the complexity of the logistics may prove to be an unbearable burden, on top of everything else.

If you are going to work for a big multinational or employer, they may be able to help you with the relocation process by shipping a certain amount of your possessions free of charge. If not, they may still be able to recommend reliable relocation services.

Similarly, recruitment firms are increasingly offering relocation services as part of the overall package when finding jobs abroad for their clients.

If travelling further than Europe, you could use a professional removals company. If so, you should hire an accredited moving firm with a good reputation.

# Immigration paperwork

At this stage, you have probably already checked out the immigration regulations for some countries you are thinking of moving to – and no doubt felt a pang of worry, if not panic, at the apparently dazzlingly complex visa-application process.

The good news is that patience and perseverance, and professional advice where necessary, will get you through this potential stumbling block.

## The European Union

Moving from Ireland to another country in the EU can be a frustrating contradiction: on the one hand, you do not need a visa to move to another country in the EU, but on the other hand, where you do need official documentation, European bureaucracy can be agonisingly slow and pedantic. The EU countries can be divided into three groups:

Those which do not require documentation

Those which do not officially require documentation, but where, in practice, it could be advantageous to have it

Those countries which require documentation

## Who can help?

In general, because of the fact that EU nationals do not have to qualify to live in another EU country, there are few professionals to assist with immigration. The biggest challenge you are likely to face is in translating essential documents like birth and marriage certificates and employment and accommodation contracts.

While local registered translators and translation companies will probably be available, you may also start your search by checking out the website of the European Union of Associations of Translation Companies (*www.eutac.org*), which has links to the national translation associations of France, Spain, Portugal, Germany and Italy.

## Outside the EU

The immigration systems of Australia, New Zealand, Canada and America are essentially divided into three similar categories: skilled, business, and family.

SKILLED For those with skills in demand. In America, this category is called 'Employment-Based'; in Australia, it is the 'Skilled Stream'; in Canada, skilled and business visas are grouped together under the 'Economic Class'; and in New Zealand, it is the 'Skilled Migrant' category.

BUSINESS Typically known as 'Investor' or 'Entrepreneur' visas, for those with investment funds, business ownership or management experience.

FAMILY This area is for those with spouses or common-law partners who can apply for their partners to immigrate. Dependent children, parents and grandparents can also potentially apply to the family immigration programme.

While you do not officially need professional assistance in order to make an immigration application to Australia, New Zealand, Canada or America, it is an option well worth considering if you hate form-filling and bureaucracy, or if you have a complicated application (for example, having a criminal record).

Application fees payable to government immigration departments – that is, to the government of the country in question, not to the professional you might hire to help – range from hundreds to, in the case of some business applications, thousands of euro.

## Who can help?

Although similar, the regulations covering professional assistance in Australia, New Zealand, Canada and America are by no means identical. Here are details of who can help:

| | |
|---|---|
| AUSTRALIA | Migration lawyers and migration agents |
| NEW ZEALAND | Immigration advisors |
| AMERICA | Immigration attorneys and business consultants |
| CANADA | Immigration lawyers and consultants. |

It is worth checking to ensure that your professional advisor is covered by professional indemnity insurance. Professional indemnity insurance protects you and gives you a platform from which to seek recompense.

## Immigration changes

Immigration departments often make changes on an annual basis, or following a change in government. Sometimes, changes are made retroactively, invalidating an application already in progress. Always keep up to date with the latest regulations and criteria affecting your preferred destinations.

# Financial advice

It may also be worthwhile seeking professional advice for moving your finances. Depending on the extent of your resources, how and when you move your money and investments abroad are concerns on which an authorised advisor may offer some valuable guidance.

## Currency exchange

If you are moving outside the EU, you will need to arrange for your euro to be changed into the local currency of your destination. However, it is not as simple as changing all your funds into the new currency. Since you are moving lock, stock and barrel, you may have tens of thousands of euro to change, and even a minor fluctuation in exchange rates may affect the value of your funds considerably.

There are two main ways to minimise these exchange-rate risks: watch the markets closely, then transfer money via a bank when the time is right, or use a foreign exchange (FOREX) specialist.

If you choose to transfer the money yourself at an opportune moment, you will need access to your funds at short notice – something that is not always possible. This approach will also require considerable time spent monitoring the markets. Additionally, you may only be offered the tourist rate of exchange. Approach the bank directly to try and negotiate a more competitive rate, and you may be able to strike a good deal.

However, if you take the second option of using a FOREX specialist, you are likely to secure a better rate than the bank will offer.

When choosing a company to help you change currency, follow these tips:

Check on the websites of companies dealing in currency. Some publish their rates online; others will make them available after registration.

Request information on additional charges for providing the service and how long they take to transfer money on their clients' behalf.

Find out how long they have been in business and how many big clients they have: the more money they transfer generally, the more competitive rate they should be able to offer in your case.

Ask if they have indemnity insurance for their staff.

## Banking overseas

Unless you are being relocated by a new employer or have hired a relocation expert in your new home, you will have to make the decision who to bank with yourself.

The key differences between banking in Ireland and abroad are:

TERMINOLOGY  In Ireland, we have banks, building societies and credit unions, but abroad you will also find commercials, co-operatives, thrifts, and other names for banks. Mostly, though, they will function like a typical Irish bank, with either current or savings accounts.

CHEQUES  These are not so widely used abroad. While common in France, they are almost unheard of in Scandinavian countries.

CHARGES  Bank charges can be higher in many countries overseas, whether it is routine administration charges for banking transactions or penalties for unauthorised overdrafts.

ASSORTED PRODUCTS  Banks abroad sometimes sell a wider range of products than simply offering financial services. If you need to buy a bicycle in Spain, for example, a bank may be the answer . . . whereas it's not unheard of for banks in some parts of the US to run gun-purchase promotions.

The European Central Bank publishes information about interest rates offered by banks and other financial institutions in EU countries on its website, *www.ecb.int.*

## Authorised Advisor

An authorised advisor offers independent financial advice. You can check the regulatory status of any firm with the Financial Regulator (*www.financialregulator.ie*), who can also provide information about investment firms and money transmitters/bureaux de change.

## Financial services outside of the EU

Evaluating the advantages and disadvantages of moving financial assets, such as a pension, to a country outside the EEA requires an assessment of the tax regimes of both Ireland and the country in question. For certain and clear guidance, consult experts who can advise on both jurisdictions. There are three ways of doing this:

> Find a person or group with investment knowledge of both countries in question. If you can identify an Irish authorised advisor who emigrated recently and has since become a financial adviser overseas, they would be ideal.

> Consult an Irish authorised advisor who works with an authorised advisor/independent financial advisor in your country of destination.

> Talk to an international firm with expertise in both jurisdictions applicable to you.

# Buying property

## Estate Agents

Although it is always tempting to search for your own property, thereby avoiding agents' fees, it is worth remembering that a good agent knows the local marketplace and which developers are trustworthy.

## How to find a good estate agent

Regulatory and licensing frameworks differ from country to country, so finding a good estate agent will require you to research what membership licensing and accreditation an agency has. You should also check what protection to the consumer is afforded by trade accreditation.

Membership of an accreditation body is no guarantee of good service, although it does mean that you'll have a forum to make an official complaint in the event of poor service.

It goes without saying that buying property is a major investment, so good advice from a professional estate agent is vital in ensuring a successful investment. As well as taking every precaution you can to ensure that your estate agent is reputable, avoid chance or risky transactions. Never buy sight unseen, and never rush into a commitment, especially if you are being pressured to make your move immediately.

When enlisting the services of an estate agent, you are likely to encounter local procedures and differences in terminology from the Irish equivalent. Here's a list of key points:

TERMINOLOGY AND LANGUAGE There are the obvious differences in language, but even in English-speaking countries, confusion arises from an array of property types being named differently.

SIZE Overseas, properties are often listed by size in square metres, rather than by number of bedrooms.

FEATURES Each country has different architectural standards and styles: many Canadian homes have large basements, many New Zealand homes have no central heating, many Spanish homes have tiled floors, and many Norwegian homes are made from wood.

TERMINOLOGY  Estate agents are called different things in different countries:

| | |
|---|---|
| France | *Agent immobilier* |
| Spain | *Agents de fincas* |
| Portugal | *Mediador autorizado* |
| Germany | *Makler, immobilienmakler* or *wohnungsmakler* |
| Australia | *Estate agent* |
| New Zealand | *Real-estate agent* |
| Canada | *Real-estate broker* or *realtor* |
| America | *Real-estate agent, realtor* or *realtist* |

## Mortgages

Again, unless you're a Lottery winner or have emerged from the Celtic Tiger crash unscathed, buying a home overseas is likely to involve getting a suitable mortgage. You can arrange this by doing research to find the best lenders or by employing a professional to do this for you. Here are some important differences between Irish and overseas mortgages:

Mortgages are either granted on the basis of a multiple of your salary, or as a percentage of your net monthly income. (In Europe, this typically ranges from 30 to 33 percent.)

The maximum loan-to-value mortgage is usually lower in Europe than it is in Ireland (typically 60 to 80 percent as opposed to 85 to 90 percent).

Loans are available in some countries to make up the shortfall between the mortgage and the purchase price.

Terms in most EU countries are typically fifteen years, as opposed to the twenty-five-year standard in Ireland and the twenty-five- to thirty-year terms common in Australia, New Zealand, Canada and America.

The range of available mortgages differs, and repayment mortgages are the norm in the EU.

## Mortgage brokers

When looking for help with a mortgage in your new country, the best option is to enlist a good, well-established mortgage broker.

Just like in Ireland, a good broker overseas will evaluate your individual circumstances and advise on how much you can borrow and the type of mortgage that is best for you.

It must be kept in mind, though, that many mortgage brokers receive a commission from the lenders. Therefore, you'll want to feel confident that you're getting the right advice for you, and not the advice that is right for the broker to give. Again, this will entail some local research, as the regulation of mortgage brokers is piecemeal. The role of some official associations, as is the case in America and Canada, are more educational and informative than regulatory. In Australia and New Zealand, the professional mortgage brokers' association requires individual brokers to have professional indemnity insurance. In France and Spain, by contrast, some brokers have professional indemnity insurance and some do not.

## Mortgages: What to do and what not to do

Some of these tips are just common sense and would apply to dealing with an insurance broker in Ireland as well as abroad.

### WHAT TO DO

Shop around and compare rates and prices. It's usually a bad sign if a broker or lender is putting you under pressure to act quickly or to use them instead of others.

Ask what association the broker belongs to and check whether a condition of membership is professional indemnity insurance. If it is, the broker is covered against any compensation claims, and if there is any proven wrongdoing, you'll be able to get your money back.

Keep an eye on the paperwork throughout the process to make sure that the charges and loan terms are as mutually agreed.

Be realistic, and above all be honest with yourself and the broker, when working out how much you think you can afford to borrow. You don't want your new life to begin under the burden of excessive financial pressure.

WHAT NOT TO DO
Sign contracts or documents without checking them thoroughly and reading the small print.

Lie about your financial situation in order to get a loan.

Borrow more money than you know you can afford to repay.

## The purchase process
The first step to purchasing a property abroad is similar to buying a home in Ireland: you have to arrange your budget with a mortgage lender, and identify a property you can afford.

Next, you have to agree a price with a seller and draw up a legally binding contract. Before putting pen to paper, you'll want a professional and independent appraisal of the document to ensure that it's all above board.

Then comes 'conveyance'. Just as in Ireland, this entails your solicitor checking that the title deeds are in order, arranging the registration of the title, recording the sale, and ensuring that all taxes and government and municipal charges have been paid by the previous owner. This is handed by a solicitor – normally a lawyer who specialises in conveyance.

In most counties, using a specialist conveyancer – whether they are called a solicitor, lawyer or notary – is obligatory.

## What is a notary?

Notaries are public officials qualified in civil law who often handle conveyancing. While a notary may also be involved in drafting the initial contracts, be aware that notaries do not act in an advisory capacity, so do not consider their input to be independent legal advice.

The Council of the Notariats of the European Union represents notaries in France, Spain, Portugal, Italy and Germany, as well as several other countries. Its website, *www.cnue.be*, has links to the national bodies.

## Deposits

Generally, deposits are only refundable where conditions in the preliminary contract were not met within the time-frame laid out. It is imperative that your lawyer ensures that the contract clearly specifies how the deposit is being offered. It is essential to have clarity in this regard, especially to avoid a breach of contract, for which you may be fined a considerable amount.

Always transfer the deposit to the lawyer or conveyancing specialist handling the sale for you rather than directly to a seller. Only lodge the money with an estate agent if they are fully bonded and accredited.

## What next?

Spend some time on your homework before you employ someone and make sure that you understand what you want from them.

Check credentials and references. You want to feel as confident as you possibly can that the professional will deliver for you.

When considering using an overseas professional, compare their services to the standard services offered in Ireland. If the professional overseas seems to offer a lesser service, try to identify the reason for this. It could be because of a difference in law or local regulations. Also, ask a trusted Irish professional whether they can provide the services for you.

Keep up to date with the paperwork and all the goings-on so that you can step in if anything happens that you are uncomfortable about or unhappy with.

Once you have decided whether you can go it alone in organising your move abroad, or whether you need the help of professionals, it's time to start thinking about wrapping up your Irish affairs.

# 5

# Wrapping Up Your Irish Affairs

Having undertaken solid groundwork for your move abroad, your mind might be focused on starting over on new soil. But I'm afraid there's plenty left for you to do in Ireland yet, such as arranging your finances, relocating your possessions, and getting rid of the rest.

## A clean break?

So far, the advice has been to commit to your move 100 percent and not be looking back over your shoulder at life in Ireland. This may lead you to prove your commitment by cutting all your connections with Ireland. But while committing fully to your move, it's also sensible to leave a door open for your return. And selling your home (if you own one) and closing all your bank accounts will make returning to Ireland a much trickier process, should you need to do so.

### Selling your home

Chances are that if you're a home owner, you'll be looking to fund your emigration by selling your property. You won't need to be told that the Irish market is fairly stagnant at the moment, with credit lines severely restricted and people having little confidence about making major financial investments.

It isn't a sellers market, and doesn't look like it will be anytime soon. If you're thinking of selling anyway, it could be a good idea to put up the 'For Sale' signs well in advance of your planned move.

How long it takes to sell your home, and what price you achieve, will have an impact on the timing of your move abroad and how much money you have for accommodation overseas. Three things to consider are:

Avoid selling in haste and way below market value.

Get expert advice on how to make a quick sale at the asking price.

Let the property until the market picks up and your target sale price is likely to be met.

There is no clear-cut right or wrong answer as to whether to sell your property, but the sluggish Irish property market might take the matter out of your hands. If you plan to hang on to your Irish home, will you still be able to afford to relocate to another country? If not, perhaps the timing just isn't right for you to emigrate.

## Letting your home

If you want to consider letting your home, think about the following:

Who is your typical tenant likely to be, how long will they rent for, and how much are they likely to pay?

Will your property need to be decorated or adapted for letting purposes?

Where is the most effective place for you to advertise? How long before you leave should you advertise?

Can you ask a friend or relative to manage the lettings for you while you are away, or will you employ an agency to handle it for you? If you choose to use a lettings agency, find out what their take is, and if they can guarantee an income regardless of occupancy.

How will letting your property affect your tax, and will letting out an Irish property result in you being defined as 'ordinarily resident' in Ireland? The Revenue will give definitive answers to this.

Ideally, you'll get enough in rent to cover your mortgage and upkeep costs. If not, is it really worth letting your home to a stranger?

Location, location, location. Is your home in a good neighbourhood, close to city businesses or commuter routes? If not, your property may not be in demand and finding a suitable tenant may prove difficult.

## Selling your car

The market for second-hand car sales, just like the housing market, is stagnant. You may be able to make a quick sale to family or friends. If you're going through the classified and advertising route, factor in enough time to sell the car.

# Getting the timing right

Choosing the ideal time to make your move from Ireland is not an easy decision. The amount of time you think it will take to wrap up your affairs, as well as selling or letting your house and working out your employment notice, will all play a part in your judgement.

If you've ever left a job, you'll notice that the 'to do' list gets longer and longer as the number of days left to work get shorter. The same thing happens when you're moving. As emigrating is a bigger move than most, the list really does get very long. So the last few weeks before you set sail will probably be a little frantic, despite your best intentions and planning.

The flip side to this, though, is wrapping up too early and finding yourself sitting at home in the dark with the electricity turned off and wearing the same clothes for too many days in a row.

Eircom, the ESB and Bord Gáis require only a couple of days' notice to close your account (you'll need to take a final metre reading before you leave and pay off any outstanding bills), so while you don't want to be overly optimistic when planning your departure date, there is room for flexibility.

When writing your 'to do' list, start with your planned departure date and then work back, making a note of all the things you need to do by then.

# Countdown to departure

### One year to six months to go

If you haven't travelled in a while, check that your passport is valid and up to date, and will have at least six months to run after you plan to leave.

Track the progress of your visa application to gauge whether it will be ready when you are.

If taking a pet with you, research what inoculations, paperwork and quarantine procedures are needed.

If nearing state pension age, contact the Revenue for an assessment of what Irish state pension you can expect.

If you plan to sell your house or let it through an agent, get a quote from at least three agencies.

Check your job contract: what notice period do you need to give?

Research and book any vaccinations you may need.

## Six months to three months to go

Inform your child's school of the child's final day.

If you'll need a removals service, get three firms to visit your house and provide an estimate of moving costs. Book your preferred movers.

Start going through your belongings, deciding what you're selling, what you'll store, and what you'll bring with you.

Make a list of all the paperwork you might need on arrival overseas, and make sure you have it all: birth certificate, employment references, exam results, and so on. It may take weeks to be issued with replacements.

Organise any specific travel or health insurance you may need.

If renting, check your contract to see how much notice you are required to give your landlord or agency, and let them know you are planning a move.

If you think you'll need it in your new country and it hasn't already been obtained for visa purposes, write to your local Garda Superintendent to request a police certificate.

## Three months to one month to go

Start packing anything that doesn't need to be packed expertly by the movers, taking care to label the contents of each box clearly.

If you haven't already, give your employer official notice of your resignation.

Apply for E104 and E301 forms from the Department of Social Welfare, proving your employment history in Ireland and your Irish social insurance records.

Arrange a place to stay on arrival, so you'll have a forward address for any important or urgent mail.

## One month to two weeks to go

Notify the following organisations of your move:

Revenue

Social security

Legal and financial services (such as banks, credit card companies, and so on)

Your local GP and dentist

Clubs and organisations you belong to

Publications you subscribe to

Any local businesses you have an account with

An Post (and ask about their international redirection service).

Arrange for transport to the airport on your day of departure.

## Final week

Check that all the documentation you are taking with you is complete.

Arrange for your utilities to be turned off, and settle your accounts. Check tax and social security contributions for a possible rebate.

Cancel all regular payments from your bank accounts.

Pay any other outstanding bills.

Finish packing your belongings.

Say your goodbyes.

## Departure day

Take final utilities reading and request final bills.

Request final bills from your telecoms and television companies, as applicable.

Leave keys to your property with your estate agent, rental agent or family.

Ensure that all important documents and emergency numbers are accessible.

# Finance

The excitement of living in a new country, working in a new job and meeting new people are probably to the fore – but don't neglect the financial nuts and bolts of money, taxes and pensions, or you could leave yourself short of cash and credit.

## Employment records and benefits

You can prove your employment history in Ireland and your Irish social insurance records through forms E104 and E301. You should obtain these documents before you leave Ireland in order to apply for sickness or unemployment benefits abroad. They will also help you qualify for other social payments, such as the state pension.

You can download the application form to request the E104 and E301 forms at *www.welfare.ie/EN/Forms/Documents/e301.pdf.* Complete the form and send it to the EU Record Section of the Department of Social and Family Affairs. You must include copies of your P45 (from the current and previous tax years) and a copy of your P60 from the previous tax year.

Processing your application can take a few months. You may contact the International Record Section by phone one month after you submit your application.

## Transferring welfare benefits

If you are getting Jobseeker's Benefit, your claim may be transferred to another EEA member state for up to thirteen weeks, if you are looking for work there. You must be getting Jobseeker's Benefit for at least four weeks before the date of your departure; you may still be allowed to transfer your payment if you get a written letter from FÁS stating that you are unlikely to secure full-time employment in this country in the foreseeable future. You will need to complete Form E303 from your local social welfare office and take it to the social services of the country you are travelling to. Means-tested payments, such as Jobseeker's Allowance or Supplementary Welfare Allowance, cannot be transferred to another EU/EEA country.

## PPS number

You will not need to give up your PPS number, as it is a unique reference number given to you for life. You will be able to use it even if you come back to Ireland after many years.

## Voting Abroad

On the whole, Irish citizens living abroad cannot vote in an election or referendum here in Ireland. The only real exceptions to this are those who are eligible for postal voting: full-time members of the Garda Síochána and the Defence Forces, and Irish diplomats posted abroad.

However, for European Parliament elections, if you are currently living in an EU country and are registered to vote in that country, you are entitled to vote for your local European Parliament candidates wherever you are living.

## Transferring your assets

Your move abroad will inevitably mean resolving some complex money issues, such as what to do with any Irish-based pensions, investments or savings.

## Tax

If you are unemployed when leaving Ireland, you may be entitled to a tax refund. If tax has been deducted from your pay since 1 January and you haven't used all of your tax credits, you may be entitled to a tax rebate. For more details, contact your local Revenue office (see *www.revenue.ie/en/contact/index.html*).

## Working in the EU

By working in another member state and transferring your residence there, you are likely to become 'resident for tax purposes' in that country. In general, you are subject to income tax in the country where you are living. The laws on personal taxation vary considerably from one member state to another, and you may be liable for taxation in more than one country. Tax agreements between most of the member states of the EU are intended to avoid double taxation, if you derive income from different countries.

France, Spain, Portugal, Italy, Germany, Australia, New Zealand, Canada and America have double-taxation treaties with Ireland. This will be significant if you are resident in one of these countries while receiving earnings or profits from Ireland. In such cases, you may find that you are obliged to pay tax on the gain where you reside, but also in the country where the gain was made. As being taxed twice is unfair, bilateral double taxation agreeements often require that tax be paid in the country of residence but not in the country in which it arises. Alternatively, the country where the gain arises may deduct the tax at source, with the taxpayer receiving a compensating foreign tax credit in the country of residence.

# Pensions

## Preparation

If you're contributing to more than one pension, the expertise of a financial advisor will give you a clear estimation of what your pension income abroad is likely to be. They will also advise on queries such as:

Can you continue to contribute to your Irish pension from overseas?

What are the tax implications of doing so?

Can you claim a pension overseas?

Should you transfer an Irish-based pension to an investment scheme in your new country of residence, or should you keep your pensions in Ireland?

## Continuing contributions

If you are under pension age, ask your advisor about continuing to pay voluntary health contributions while living overseas in order to receive the full Irish state pension.

A person who works and pays social insurance in another EU country or in a country with which Ireland has a bilateral agreement can have social insurance aggregated with social insurance paid in Ireland to qualify for a state pension (contributory). A pension entitlement determined in this way is a pro-rata payment based on the proportion of Irish social insurance contributions to the total number of contributions paid and/or credited (Irish and other insurance combined).

Ireland has bilateral agreements with USA, Canada, Quebec (which has a separate system from the rest of Canada), Australia, New Zealand, the UK (including the Channel Islands and Isle of Man), Austria, Switzerland and Korea.

You should be able to remain in any Irish private or work-related pension schemes of which you are a member as long as the rules of the scheme allows it. However, the pension's value may be affected by tax and inflation, so consult your authorised financial advisor.

## Claiming your pensions

You can claim your Irish state pension in any European Economic Area country, as well as the countries with which Ireland has bilateral agreements, and you will get the same income as you would if you had stayed in Ireland.

If you pay sufficient contributions into a scheme in your new country, you should be eligible for a pension there as well.

If your Irish-based pension is paid in euro and you are outside of the EU, it will need to be exchanged for the local currency – exposing it to the prevailing exchange rates (something which may or may not run in your favour).

## Moving your pension overseas

Cashing in on your Irish pension and moving the funds to your new home may be an option – but is likely to be a detrimental one. Early redemption penalties, taxation and differing interest rates are all factors that could have a negative impact on the value of your investment. Seek professional advice before moving such an important investment.

## Removals

Moving lock, stock and barrel is a big physical undertaking. Depending on where you are moving, and how much you intend to bring, moving your possessions may be something you can take care of yourself.

If you need professional help, you'll want to identify a company that specialises in international removals. Check that your chosen removals firm is a member of the Fédération Internationale des Déménageurs Internationaux (FIDI) or the Overseas Moving Network International (OMNI).

You should shop around and ask for quotations from three firms. They are quite keen for business, and most offer estimates free of charge.

The cost will depend on whether you need less-than-container-load or full-container-load services:

LESS THAN CONTAINER LOAD (LCL) If your things do not fill up the whole shipping container, you can ask to consolidate your goods with another shipper's goods inside the same container.

FULL CONTAINER LOAD (FCL) Most customers select either a twenty-foot or a forty-foot container to move their household goods and personal effects.

'Groupage' service refers to a shipping container that is loaded with personal-effects shipments other than your own. When there are sufficient goods to fill the container, it is then booked on a vessel. This consolidation of shipments usually takes between one and four weeks, depending on how much cargo is already available, and on the time of year.

Most Irish-based international removal firms include the following in their service: pick up from residence and port/airport; documentation; transport by sea, air or land; insurance; shipment tracking; Customs clearance; and delivery to your new home.

## Cars

If you are thinking of bringing your car, check with the appropriate authority in the country you are moving to what the requirements are. In some European countries, you will have to have compliance tests, and there may be bureaucratic hassle in legally registering the vehicle. And don't forget that in most EU countries, cars are left-hand drive.

## Choosing a removals company

The major factor in your choice of removals firm could be timing. Removal companies usually require at least a month's notice of your departure date. Summer tends to be the busiest period, so if you want to move then, moving companies may not be able to facilitate your preferred date. However, once a date is agreed, experienced companies are often flexible enough to put off your departure date if unexpected problems crop up, such as delays in your visa.

NINE QUESTIONS TO ASK A REMOVALS COMPANY

Do you have accreditation?

Which removals company will be dealing with my possessions in the destination? Are they accredited?

How will my possessions be transported?

Do you provide packing materials? If so, does it cost extra?

How much preparation will I be expected to do?

Do you dismantle furniture and take down curtains free of charge? If not, what is the charge?

Will it save me money if I pack everything myself?

Do fragile and oddly shaped items cost more to pack?

Can I provide my own evaluation for insurance purposes?

## Insurance

International removals companies typically offer insurance at 3 percent of the value of the goods being shipped. It is important, therefore, that you agree with the valuation. You will also want to check whether this is being included in your estimate or whether it is charged separately. Some independent commercial brokers who specialise in marine insurance may be able to offer a cheaper deal, although the coverage may be less comprehensive.

## Importation duties and paperwork

The requirements for duty and documentation differ from country to country, but your chosen removal firm will be able to advise you on how to negotiate Customs when bringing your possessions into the country, and may include this as part of their service.

### Duty

EU  No duty or taxes will be payable on your imported possessions.

Australia, New Zealand, Canada, America  No duty is payable on items that have been owned and used abroad for more than twelve months preceding the owner's arrival into the country. If the goods are newer, they may

79

be subject to duty charges. You may have to prove this with receipts.

### DOCUMENTATION FOR HOUSEHOLD GOODS

In the EU, Australia, New Zealand and America, a photocopy of the photograph and visa pages of your passport must be attached to your inventory list. Canadian Customs officials will want to see your actual passport.

Some countries will require a Customs declaration form, but again, an international removal firm should be able to advise you on the requirements.

## What to ship

You never really know just how much you own until you move home. Even if you live in a minimalist style in a one-bedroom flat, clear it out and you'll be surprised by how many things you have. And as you rediscover those LPs you stacked under the bed, or the complete Jack Kerouac collection you've been keeping safe in a box, you'll wonder how you could ever be parted from such treasures.

Thus begins the heart-wrenching battle between practical and sentimental belongings!

It's always gut-wrenching to leave behind stuff that has a strong emotional attachment, but speaking from experience, in the long run it pays to be as objective as possible. You can only bring so much, and the more you bring, the more it will cost you. As you take stock, item by item, the choice can be stark: do you take your job-interview suit or your 1990 replica Ireland football shirt? Your head says suit, your heart says shirt . . .

Leaving possessions behind usually means selling them, giving them away (or simply chucking them out), or storing them.

For possessions you have a particularly strong emotional attachment to, ask someone you trust to store them for you. Then, when you're far away, you can have warm thoughts about your treasured items being in safe hands. Professional storage for larger items is also an option, although a costly one.

One way of turning the heartbreak of parting with your prized items into a feel-good boost is to give them away to someone who will really treasure and appreciate them. You can give yourself a pat on the back for benevolence and be content that they have found a good home.

Finally, if you can't leave your possessions with anyone, or if you want to cash in on items that have some value, try selling your goods. (Incidentally, a 1990 Ireland football top will earn you a tasty sum of cash on eBay.)

When it comes to deciding what furniture to ship, think about whether your existing furniture will suit the surroundings of your new home. How expensive will it be to buy new or second-hand furniture when you get there?

Your decision on what items to bring will probably be best made by working out how much money you'll raise by selling them, how much it will cost to replace them in your new home, and what difference they will make to the overall shipping costs.

You could even ask the removal estimators to provide a couple of quotations: one for the items you definitely need to bring, and another that includes items you are unsure about.

Bear in mind also that the shipping time to your destination could range from a day or two (for parts of France, say) to more than a month (if shipping to New Zealand, Australia and parts of Canada and America). So unless you are moving into fully furnished accommodation, buying essential items when you arrive might make a lot more sense than going without for weeks as you wait, with growing impatience, for your consignment to arrive.

When you have a list of items you are definitely taking, go over the list with your removal company. For instance, some countries, particularly Australia and New Zealand, have stringent requirements covering how to clean items and to what standard (particularly items that have come into contact with soil and vegetation).

## Electrical items

When thinking about whether it is worth taking electrical items abroad, there are three factors to consider: electrical supply, plug type and television standard.

## Paperwork

Your international removers will provide your packing inventory, which you will need to photocopy twice for Customs.

You'll also need a range of other important documents that will ensure smooth sailing, and prove useful when going about starting your new life. Here's a list of some of the most essential documents. Take two photocopies, preferably at least one set in your hand luggage:

Passport valid for at least six months

Both colour and black-and-white passport-sized photos with white background (for ID cards, applications, and so on)

Your Irish/old proof of address, such as title deeds to your home or rental property, driving licence, or utility bills

Bank statement or other proof of funds

Work contract, if applicable

Private health insurance policy, if necessary

Driving licence

Details of insurance history: number of years insured, no-claims history, and details of any claims history. This might help you obtain a better car- or home-insurance deal than would otherwise have been the case.

Education certificates and schooling records for your children, if applicable

Birth and marriage certificates

Glasses prescription

Medical and dental records

Prescription or letter from your doctor about medication you are taking with you, if applicable

CV

For your peace of mind, and particularly if you need to return, leave photocopies of the above in Ireland with a trusted family member, friend or solicitor.

## Health insurance

Those living within the European Economic Area (EEA) can apply for 'E' forms, introduced to make it possible to exercise social security and healthcare rights in other member states.

The form E106 is a certificate of entitlement to health care in another EEA country for a limited duration. When the E106 is registered, the person and registered dependants can receive medical treatment on the same basis as an insured person of the member state of residence. It entitles the holder to free health care for up to two years, but will become null and void as soon as you register with the country's social security system.

If you are moving to America, you must obtain health

insurance before you emigrate. You may also need to do so if relocating to Canada, but this depends on which province you are moving to.

## Taking your pet

The further you intend to travel, the higher the cost of moving your pet overseas. Depending on where you are headed, the cost of vaccinations and micro-chipping could rise from several hundred to a few thousand euro. The correct vaccinations are crucial if you are to avoid your pet ending up in quarantine. Don't forget to bring your pet's health records, particularly its vaccination history.

If you can't afford to take your pet, or find that doing so is impractical, set about finding them a caring new home as early as possible. Many pet shelters have noted a sharp rise in the number of pets being abandoned in the credit crunch, as owners move away or downsize to smaller apartments. If you can't find a suitable home for your pet, you may find the shelters nearest you are full, so act early and don't neglect your duty of care.

## Packing your personal luggage

As finding employment is likely to be a priority, bring enough smart clothes for you to attend interviews looking well and feeling confident. Similarly, if you have a job lined up, check with your employer what clothes are suitable for the workplace, and pack accordingly.

You should also pack some clothes at the other end of the spectrum – work-wear and casual clothing you can use when it comes to the physical nitty-gritty of things to do during the settling-in period.

Most importantly, don't forget that overweight bags incur prohibitive surcharges – so check the weight restrictions in advance and avoid going over the top.

## Child's play

If you think long journeys are uncomfortable and boring, spare a thought for your children. A few new toys or colouring books could make all the difference in ensuring that everyone has a good journey.

## What next?

Hopefully the issues raised in this chapter will enable you to wrap up your Irish affairs in a sensible and timely fashion. Think about:

the issues that will affect the timing of your planned departure

how much of a clean break you want to make

arranging for your possessions to be moved or disposed of

arranging your finances prior to moving

ways in which you can cope with potentially stressful situations.

# 6

# Relocation

## Arrival

The scale of the immigration processes you need to complete on arrival depends on the country you move to, but there are some universal requirements regardless of destination.

Whether you remain within the EU or travel further, your passport will be checked.

A move outside the EU will also entail the completion of Customs forms and a landing card, and your visa will be stamped. There is usually a limit to the amount of currency (in cash or travellers' cheques) you can import without declaring it. The limit differs in each jurisdiction, but can be easily researched online or with travel specialists.

The border agents may also ask for evidence that you have the means to fund yourself (and your family), so it is useful to have some recent bank statements with you as proof of funds.

### Getting started

As you go about starting life in your new home, you may need local help with any number of services. And unlike in Ireland, you won't have an established network of trusted or recommended tradespeople. For sound recommendations of reputable service providers, try some of the following sources, who will have local knowledge:

IMMIGRATION DEPARTMENTS  The Australian, Canadian and New Zealand immigration departments provide regionally focused settlement support. The US provides a downloadable guide and lists sources of assistance on the website *www.welcometousa.gov.*

TOWN HALLS, TOURISM OFFICES, CHAMBERS OF COMMERCE, LIBRARIES AND IRISH EMBASSIES AND CONSULATES  All can be a useful source of information on local services.

FRIENDS, FAMILY, NEIGHBOURS AND COLLEAGUES  Many emigrants find the local population to be extremely helpful, so even if you don't have friends and family to help you settle down, you are not necessarily on your own.

IRISH CENTRES  Most major cities in the US and UK have Irish support and community services who will have a trades network you can tap into.

## Relocation services

Mundane tasks that require little endeavour in Ireland, such as arranging bank accounts, utilities and mobile-phone service, can be difficult in an unfamiliar country, especially where there is a language barrier.

Local companies will offer help in everything from picking you up at the airport to finding accommodation, sometimes at an hourly rate and sometimes for a flat fee. In Australia and Canada, it is common commercial practice for any estate agent you are dealing with to consult as unofficial relocation specialist.

# Red tape

Once you have arrived and have somewhere to live, be it a temporary or a permanent home, you will need to make the local and national government departments aware of your presence.

Exactly what you need to do in order to register with the authorities depends entirely on the jurisdiction. Even under the EU umbrella, each individual country will have its own immigration bureaucracy. The following list will give you a general idea of what you need to do shortly after you arrive.

Most administrations within the EU will require you to apply for a residence permit.

Within ten days of arrival in America, you must notify the United States Citizenship and Immigration Services of your new address.

Register your residency with the local Irish embassy or consulate.

Apply for a tax number. Wherever you go, this process may take some weeks, so the sooner you apply, the better.

Also, if you're looking for work, notify the department of social security.

Register with the national health service (if applicable).

Sign up with a local doctor and dentist.

Contact the driving licence authority (if applicable).

When applying for residence in the EU, there is often a time limit in which you have to register or apply for residency. In Germany, you must register within a week of taking up residence in a private dwelling, but other EU countries allow 30, 90 or 120 days for you to apply for the appropriate permit.

Various personal documents may be asked for. These include your passport and passport-sized photos, and you may also need completed application forms, fees, proof of residence, birth certificates, marriage certificate, a record of good conduct provided by the Gardaí, evidence of financial independence and employment, bank account details and health insurance.

Permanent residence is usually a two-step process. Step one is qualifying for a residence permit; step two is applying for permanent residence after a qualifying period (usually between three and five years).

## Tax and social security

One of the most important tasks to prioritise after arrival is applying for your tax and social security number. This is vital for establishing employment and access to public health care, and in some cases is also a necessity for things like opening a bank account.

As you set about establishing yourself in the early days after your arrival, use the following questions when going about registering your presence with the authorities:

How many local and national government departments will I have to register with?

What documents and forms do I need in order to do this?

Is there a certain order in which the registrations must be carried out?

Is there a set time limit in which to complete the registrations?

## Tax residence

In most cases, emigrating is effectively moving from one tax residence to another. This means that you will have to pay tax in the country you move to.

Tax residence is defined through a number of factors, such as property ownership, the amount of time you have spent in Ireland and abroad, and your employment situation. From a taxation perspective, depending on your circumstances, you could be considered tax resident in two countries simultaneously. However, you should be able to avoid paying tax in two countries: Ireland has signed double-taxation agreements with fifty-one countries. Therefore, if you are resident in one of these countries while receiving earnings or profits from Ireland, you will effectively be taxed only once on these earnings.

The Revenue service offers comprehensive advice through the relevant section of their website, *www.revenue.ie/en/practitioner/law/tax-treaties.html*.

## Retiring to the EU

EU citizens are entitled to retire in another EU country, and the areas to prioritise in your research are what proof of funds and health care arrangements you will need.

All EU administrations will demand that you prove that you have sufficient financial means to support yourself through monthly pension payments or other income streams. Proof of your retirement income may include Irish pension, bank or investment income statements.

## Payments available from your new country

Social security benefits are available in other EEA countries once you are an employed resident contributing to the national social security scheme. But in some administrations, both within the EEA (Spain) and beyond (Australia, New Zealand, Canada and America), you need to have been paying social security contributions for a certain period before you qualify to receive benefits.

## Driving licences

Only full Irish driving licences can be used abroad: provisional licences and learner permits are not valid.

Whether or not you'll have to change your Irish driving licence for a new one depends on the country of residence. Some administrations allow your Irish licence to be valid for a certain period of time, after which you'll need to apply for a new one, while other countries allow you simply to swap your Irish licence for a local one after arrival. Check the regulations thoroughly before departing.

If you have an occupation-specific driving licence (for driving HGVs, for example), you may need to take another test in the new jurisdiction in order to continue working in that line.

# Health care

Gambling with your health by failing to pay for adequate health cover could jeopardise your entire move. Ignore this part of the emigration process at your peril.

## Health care in the EU

Ideally, you will research and organise any necessary health care cover before you move abroad. If not, you must do so as soon as possible after your arrival.

Before leaving Ireland, apply for an E106 certificate from the HSE. This is a certificate of entitlement to sickness/maternity benefits in kind for persons going to live in another member state. It is only valid temporarily – until you have become a resident or start work and sign up with social security (whichever happens first).

Private health insurance tends to be more popular in many European countries than it is in Ireland, as most of continental Europe is long used to a system of universal health insurance and a mix of public and private schemes. If you require treatment, you will have to pay costs for it. Even if you don't require medical treatment, the peace of mind that comes from knowing you will be taken care of may make the investment worthwhile.

## Health care outside the EU

The E106 is not valid outside of Europe, and no other similar reciprocal health agreements exist.

As soon as you become a permanent resident in Australia or New Zealand, you will be entitled to state-provided health care, though you should make a point of registering with the health authorities shortly after you are granted resident status.

When you are permitted to register with the health authorities in Canada depends on the regional administration. Some provincial and territorial health authorities allow you to register on arrival, thus guaranteeing immediate cover. In contrast, a three-month wait may be the standard for other authorities, and you'll have to take out private medical insurance in the meantime.

No general health care service exists in America, so you'll need to organise this yourself. If you have work arranged, they may take care of health insurance for you as one of the benefits of the job.

## Finding a doctor

What you must do to register with a GP in your new home depends on the type of health care system in place there. However, one of the following is likely to happen:

> You will be allocated a doctor following registration with social security and the national health care system.

You will be given a choice of local GPs to choose from, and are free to use any of them.

You will be given a choice of local GPs, from which you must choose one to register with.

As in Ireland, most countries will have both public and private medical clinics. And again like in Ireland, if you don't have private medical insurance, you will have to use only the public services.

# Banking and property

You'll need to arrange a bank account for the everyday transactions and purchases you require as you settle in to your new home.

## Banking

Although you can open a new bank account soon after arrival, it may take days or weeks for new credit cards and ATM cards to be issued. So it will prove useful to arrive with an Irish bank or credit card, and cash or travellers' cheques, to tide you over.

You could also try to set up a bank account before you move. This might prove tricky, as in many cases banks will only allow you to open a resident's bank account when you can prove you have the necessary visa.

However, waiting until you've emigrated before opening a bank account can have greater implications than the hassle of waiting for credit cards once you're abroad. For example, if you move to New Zealand and open an account without first obtaining an Inland Revenue Department number, you'll be charged resident's withholding tax – placing a greater burden on your budget during the initial weeks.

The best option is to contact some banks in your

planned destination before you travel, to seek their advice on making the transition as smooth as possible.

## Accommodation

Whether you plan to rent or buy a property after arrival depends on a number of factors, including your budget, exchange rates, and whether property prices are on the way up or down.

This is a decision you will have to come to by assessing your needs, making a realistic appraisal of your budget, and taking independent expert advice.

## Renting property

If you are thinking about buying a property but want to know a bit more about the area you are moving to, renting will give you the opportunity to sound out the property market, and what local amenities and transport links there are.

It will also mean that you won't be tied down to a major financial commitment in the early stage of your new life. In the event that the project doesn't work out as well as you'd hoped, or if you decide to relocate to another region in the country, renting could be the best choice for you.

However, many people consider rent 'dead money', especially if you're renting in a booming property market, and therefore have to shell out more when you do eventually decide to buy.

If you rent with a view to buying, keep an eye on property prices, as well as fluctuations in exchange rates.

## Buying property

If you have the dilemma of buying or renting, you'll want to avoid the pitfall of either buying hastily or renting for too long.

With money burning a hole in your pocket, you'll be tempted to pull the trigger and buy. And if property prices are rising sharply and are sustainable, it might make sense to buy sooner rather than later. Just as in Ireland, you should only buy when you have thorough knowledge of the area and price ranges.

## Arranging utility connections

Regardless of whether you have moved into bought or rented accommodation, you'll need to set up the utilities for your new home. The choice on offer will depend on competition in the local area. With any service, shop around where you can.

Moving into a new property may incur a reconnection fee if supplies have been disconnected in the past.

There are also differences in billing between countries. In Spain, for example, you effectively have to estimate how much electricity you think you will need. Although it is tempting to underestimate this amount, it could result in your power being cut off! Utilities to consider arranging include electricity, gas, water, telephone, broadband internet connection, television (subscription, satellite or cable), refuse collection and recycling collection.

# Settling in

As you work through your list of things to do, you'll also need to feed the more emotional aspects of your life – focusing on family, friends, and feeling good about your new home.

## Education

Finding a school for your children will depend on their age and ability and, like many other aspects of the emigration project, your budget. All of this will influence whether you enrol your child in a private or state school.

When choosing a school for your children, consider the following points:

Your child's choice of schools will depend on where you live. Religion may also be a factor.

The timetable for the academic year, term times, and the ages at which you start and finish school can vary from the Irish model. As a result, your child may have to enter an academic year that is either higher or lower than the one in which they would have been in Ireland.

If you are moving to a country where English is not the first language, you may want to check if there are any English or international schools in the area. Some schools may only teach in the native tongue, others only in English. Both have advantages and disadvantages.

## Coping with culture shock

Remember how disorientating your first day at school or in a new job was? Well, magnify some of the unfamiliarity you felt by factoring in a new language, food, culture and environment, and you'll get an idea of the feeling of culture shock often experienced within the first few days and weeks of arrival in your new home.

The feeling, though, is entirely natural. You're getting used to everything, from new social conventions to the suddenly painful absence from your life of Erin packet soup.

If you have any spare moments during these hectic days, it's inevitable that your mind will turn to thoughts or emails and phone calls with family and friends back in Ireland.

In the immediate days and weeks after your arrival, most of your time will be taken sorting through practical issues. But as you find yourself less busy and with some spare time in the evening, you should set about fulfilling your emotional needs by devoting time to establishing a new network of friends.

Keep an open mind with the people you meet on a day-to-day basis. People moving to Ireland, for instance, often find that the best way to get involved in the community is by volunteering with the local GAA club. Try to find an equivalent in your new home, whether it is a sports club or a community group.

## Employment

Your choice of destination will most likely have been influenced by the job prospects there. Ideally, your research will have entailed:

An assessment of the labour market

An evaluation of potential employers and salaries

An evaluation (and translation) of your qualifications

Steps to boost your employability, such as obtaining (or researching) any local licences that are required

Tailoring your CV to the style prevalent in the labour market in question.

The culture shock you feel will probably also be experienced in the workplace, where you may encounter different management styles or work roles.

While 'expect the unexpected' is something of a cliché, the feeling of culture shock will hopefully feel less dramatic if you acknowledge from the outset that some unsettling feelings will be coming your way.

## What next?

The weeks before and after your emigration are the busiest periods of the entire project. There are a range of tasks at hand that must all be completed, probably under the strain of saying goodbye to Ireland and settling in to a new culture.

The exact tasks depend upon your own circumstances and your destination of choice. However, your checklist may look like this:

Complete the bureaucracy of Customs, Immigration and other related departments, such as Social Security

Ensure that you (and your family, if applicable) have appropriate health care cover

Arrange your finances

Arrange somewhere to live, whether it is for the short or long term

Plan your networking and settling-in strategy in your new community.

In the following chapters, we will look in closer detail at the mechanics of emigrating to countries in Europe, the Antipodes, America, the Far East, and beyond.

# 7

# Destination UK

From the bustling multiculturalism of its cities to the rural splendour on offer in the English, Scottish or Welsh countryside, the UK continues to attract the Irish to its shores – and with the 2012 Olympics representing a major investment drive demanding a multitude of talents, many workers are turning their attention to London in particular.

## Immigration

There is free movement in the labour force between Ireland and the UK, meaning that it is not necessary to have a visa in order to work and live there on a permanent basis. However, you will need to bring identification and documents with you: photo identification (e.g. passport), records of your Irish social insurance contributions (PRSI contributions), driving licence and details of your previous car insurance cover, birth certificate, and marriage certificate (if applicable).

## Health care

If you are moving to the UK, you will be entitled to free National Health Service (NHS) hospital treatment. To access health care, you must first register with the NHS, who will provide you with an NHS number and medical card.

You may also register with your local GP, where you will be entitled to treatment. If your doctor is not available at the time of your visit, another doctor in the surgery will treat you.

There is no charge for most hospital treatment for NHS patients who live in the UK. Charges do apply for certain services, such as being given a bed in a more private location.

Although you may in theory be entitled to NHS dental treatment, you are likely to experience difficulty in finding an NHS dentist. Not all dentists treat NHS patients, while those that do may not be taking on any more patients, or may have long waiting lists for an appointment.

## Social security

The most important thing you will need to do after arrival in the UK is to apply for your National Insurance number, which works like an Irish PPS number. Your National Insurance number is your own unique reference number and ensures that the National Insurance contributions and tax you pay are properly recorded. It also acts as a reference number for the whole social security system. The type and level of National Insurance contribution you pay depends on how much you earn and whether you are employed or self-employed.

It may take up to six to eight weeks before you receive your National Insurance number. You will need this before either working or looking for benefits.

You will have to apply for a National Insurance number at a Jobcentre Plus office, where the staff will go through a process of checks with you. They will make sure that you actually need a National Insurance number, and will also confirm that you have not been supplied with one previously. Following these checks, you be called to interview, where you will be asked to prove your identity (so bring the required documents), and why you want a National Insurance number.

If you are unemployed in Ireland and in receipt of an Irish social welfare payment, you may be able to transfer your payment to the UK.

Jobseekers Benefit can be transferred to the UK for up to thirteen weeks if you are looking for employment there. To transfer this payment, you will need to have been receiving it in Ireland for at least four weeks. You will need to get Form E303 from your local social welfare office before leaving Ireland.

Note that while Jobseekers Benefit can be transferred to the UK, Jobseekers Allowance cannot.

The Jobseekers Allowance in the UK is a payment for anyone who is unemployed but capable of working. To get Jobseeker's Allowance, you also have to meet several other conditions, which include proving that you are actively looking for work.

# Taxation

Income is taxed at different rates depending on the amount of taxable income you earn. If you are working for an employer who is deducting PAYE tax and national insurance from your wages and you do not have any other income, you do not need to complete a tax return form.

Taxable income includes earnings from employment, earnings from self-employment, most income from pensions (state, company and personal pensions), interest on most savings, income from shares (dividends), rental income, and income paid to you from a trust.

Nearly everyone who is resident in the UK for tax purposes receives a 'Personal Allowance': the amount of taxable income you are allowed to earn or receive each year tax-free. After your allowable expenses and any tax-free allowances have been taken into account, the amount of tax you pay is calculated using different tax rates and a series of tax bands.

# Employment

With over a thousand offices throughout England, Wales and Scotland, the public employment service Jobcentre Plus has the largest jobs database in the UK.

Jobcentre Plus offices offer access to jobs, training opportunities and benefits for any person who is of working age and looking for work.

The National Academic Recognition Information Centre for the UK will assess your qualifications for you and give you a letter of comparability (stating how your Irish qualifications compare to UK qualifications). There is a fee for this service.

# Banking and finance

Most wages and benefits in the UK are paid directly into bank accounts, so you'll need to open a UK bank account.

The choices on offer range from banks, building societies, and online banks, and most of the names of the high-street banks will be familiar. To open an account, you'll be asked to prove your identity and address.

You might want to consider keeping your Irish account open for a while, particularly if you can use your ATM card in the UK. This will save you having to carry large amounts of cash with you. With the fall in the value of sterling, exchange rates are as favourable in 2009 as they have been for some years previously.

# Accommodation

Finding suitable accommodation should be a priority when you move to the UK. It will be easier to apply for a National Insurance number, claim benefits and find a job when you have an address.

You can arrange rented accommodation either privately with landlords or through a lettings agency. If an agency offers you accommodation, you should inspect the property before accepting the offer. You will also need to find out:

The terms and condition of the tenancy agreement

Whether your rent includes services, fuel and water charges

How much rent is required in advance

If a deposit is required, and how much

The name, address and telephone contact details of the landlord

In Scotland, whether the landlord is registered. All private landlords in Scotland should be registered with the relevant local authority.

You may have to pay a holding deposit directly to a landlord or letting agency when you agree to rent a property but have not yet taken up the tenancy. This deposit will probably be deducted from the security deposit you pay when you move into the property. In most letting arrangements, tenants have to pay a security deposit to a landlord or letting agency in case of damage to property or rent owed. You should always check the condition of the property and its contents carefully to make sure you're not charged for anything at the end of your lease that was already broken when you moved in. If the property and its contents are in the same condition as when you moved in, and you don't owe any rent, your security deposit should be returned to you.

Don't hand over any payments unless you are sure you want to move in, as a holding deposit will only be returned if you are unable to move in for reasons beyond your control. Even then, it may be difficult to get your money back.

## Property market: how to buy, and mortgages

The UK property market has suffered in recent years. The most popular location is south--east England, and London in particular, where property prices are consistently high.

Stamp Duty is lower than in Ireland, and if you purchase a property for less than £125,000, there will be no stamp duty. If you purchase below the stamp-duty threshold, your only transaction cost will be your legal fees. Solicitors can cost about £1,000 to £1,500, including all your disbursements and legal search fees.

When scouring for properties, remember that list prices are developer-driven, and they always tend to price at the top of the range. Just because you are offered a 10 percent discount doesn't mean that you are getting a bargain.

As a general rule, you can expect 80 percent loan to value when purchasing a UK property, but the UK mortgage market is one of the most sophisticated in the world. It offers a choice of around four thousand products to customers, and although credit is harder to come by these days, mortgage brokers will be keen to devise a mortgage to suit your circumstances.

## Property taxes

Council Tax/Poll Tax is a system of local taxation col-
lected by local authorities. It is a tax on domestic property. Generally, the bigger the property, the more tax will
be charged. You can expect your council tax bill by the
end of April each year.

# Utilities

ELECTRICITY There may be a number of electricity service
providers, depending on the area in which you live. With
at least two to chose from, you should shop around for
the best rates.

GAS Most major cities in the UK have a mains gas supply.

WATER There is huge demand on the water supply all
over the UK, and particularly in the south-east, where
water shortages occur regularly each summer. Accordingly, water rates are on the rise, to cover the cost of re-
newing water pipes and treatment plants. Rates do
differ, however. There are two ways that you can be
charged for your water supply, depending on whether
your property is metered or unmetered. Which is the
most cost-effective option for you depends on where
you'll be living:

> If you have a water meter, you will only pay for the
> units of water you actually use. Readings are taken
> from your meter every six months. You will also pay a
> standing charge to cover meter reading and billing
> services, usually a fixed amount each year.

> If you do not have a meter, you will pay a set rate for
> your water based on the rateable value (RV) of your
> home in England and Wales, or your council tax band if

you live in Scotland. These rates also include a standing charge to cover customer services such as billing.

TELEPHONE  A number of services and tariffs are on offer, although you may initially have to arrange for British Telecom to install your landline.

TELEVISION  A television licence system is enforced in the UK to pay for public-sector broadcasting. The 2009 TV licence fee is £142.50 for a colour television set and £48.00 for a black-and-white set.

## Education

In the UK, all children have the right to a place in school between the ages of five and sixteen.

If you are thinking of moving to the UK, you should start planning ahead. For popular schools, it is a good idea to apply more than a year in advance.

When you are enrolling your child, your first point of contact will be your Local Education Authority (LEA). The LEA is legally obliged to offer your child a place in a school. You may ask them to place your child in a particular school, but that place is not guaranteed.

Most schools in the UK are free. Over 90 percent of pupils go to state schools, which are funded by the government. There are also around 2,200 private fee-paying schools, which are independent and receive no money from the government.

## Driving

No charges apply to a car brought from Ireland to the UK as long as the car is more than six months old and has travelled more than six thousand kilometres. You can also continue to drive using your Irish licence.

# Useful websites

To get a National Insurance number:
*www.jobcentreplus.gov.uk*

For UK government services:
*www.direct.gov.uk/Homepage/fs/en*

Federation of Irish Societies:
*www.irishsocieties.org*

UK embassy in Dublin:
*www.britishembassy.ie*

EMPLOYMENT

*www.jobserve.com*
*www.fish4.co.uk/iad/jobs*
*www.jobs.co.uk*
*www.totaljobs.com*

ACCOMMODATION

*www.yha.org.uk*
*www.roomsforlet.co.uk*
*www.flat2share.co.uk*
*www.hotproperty.co.uk/renting*
*www.rentright.co.uk*

# 8

# Destination America

America has in the past welcomed countless Irish people and, while immigration controls today are restrictive, in the Irish psyche the United States continues to be seen as a unique land of opportunity. And with its vastly diverse climate, culture and landscape, America offers the potential for you to fulfil virtually any lifestyle ambition.

## Immigration

The United States Citizenship and Immigration Services (USCIS) manage American immigration. In Ireland, the USCIS works with the US Embassy in Dublin, which is responsible for issuing visas to Irish residents after an application is processed and medical and police checks have been completed.

America's immigration system grants two main types of visas: immigrant (or permanent) and non-immigrant (or temporary). An immigrant visa is the one to apply for if you want to move to America, as it provides a Permanent Residence Card, also known as a Green Card.

### Immigrant visas
The immigrant classification is in two streams: employment-based and family. These are divided into further sections, which are then broken down into sub-sections.

For example, there are five main 'employment-based' (EB) visas:

EB-1 is for 'priority workers' – those with extraordinary abilities in the sciences, arts, education, business or athletics. Applicants in this category must have extensive documentation showing sustained national or international acclaim and recognition in their field of expertise.

EB-2 is for those professionals with advanced degrees or exceptional ability in the sciences, arts or business. 'Exceptional ability' means having a degree of expertise significantly above that ordinarily encountered within the field.

EB-3 is for 'professional', 'skilled' and 'other' workers capable of performing a job requiring at least two years' training or experience.

EB-4 is for religious workers and ex-US government workers.

EB-5 is a 'job-creation' visa (though there is no work requirement) for those with at least $500,000 to invest. It is sometimes used as an option by those looking to retire in America.

Where immigration is dependent on a job offer, the prospective employer must sometimes prove to the Department of Labor that no similarly qualified US citizen or permanent resident is available to take the job. This process is called Labor Certification.

For more information on which occupations require Labor Certification, check the website *www.dol.gov*. The website *www.uscis.gov* has information on the specific categories of immigrant visas, including the schedule of fees for each type of application.

Detailed information on immigrant visas is also available at the US Embassy in Dublin: *http://dublin.us embassy.gov/*.

Family visas provide a means for spouses, parents, step-parents and children or stepchildren under the age of twenty-one to join their American relative on a permanent basis. However, these applications can take a long time to be granted – from twelve months to seven years. You can check the current waiting period of any particular visa category at the Department of State's website, *www.travel.state.gov/visa.*

Immigrant visas can be valid for a set period of time (usually between four and six months) from the date of issue, which means that you must enter the USA within this period after you receive the visa.

## The Diversity Visa Lottery Program

The Diversity Visa Lottery Program is administered on an annual basis by the Department of State. Every year, the USA Visa Lottery Program provides fifty thousand visas worldwide to natives of certain countries. A computer-generated random lottery draw chooses selected applicants. The lottery normally runs between October and December each year. Applicants must apply online at *www.dvlottery.state.gov.*

## Non-immigrant visas

The non-immigrant class visa is required by people who are visiting America on holiday or for business, as well as for temporary employment.

Working in the States on a non-immigrant employment visa sometimes makes it easier to get an employment-based visa, in that you are in a better position to capitalise on any opportunities that may arise.

# Social security and health care

Permanent residents in America must contribute to the social security system; employee contributions to the Social Security Administration are deducted at source, but the self-employed must make their own contributions.

The US government keeps track of these contributions via a Social Security number (SSN), which functions in exactly the same way as an Irish PPS number, but will also be used when you open a bank account or enrol your children in school.

When you apply for an immigrant visa, you can also request an SSN number. Within three weeks of your arrival, the SSN card will be sent to the same address to which USCIS sends your Permanent Resident Card/Green Card.

Alternatively, you can get an SSN by calling in to your local social security office with a birth certificate, passport, and visa or Green Card. It will take about two weeks for your social security card to be issued.

Social security contributions are used to fund Medicare, America's public health system. The USA does not have the same kind of state-provided public health care services found in Ireland and Europe. The actual funding is quite small, meaning that Medicare and the Medicaid programme only pays for the hospital treatment of people on very low incomes.

The cost of medical attention and hospital treatment is very expensive: a visit to a doctor (GP) can cost $100 or more. Personal health insurance is therefore essential, and most America citizens and permanent residents have private health insurance. Many employers offer this as a benefit to their employees. However, depending both on the cover you have and the treatment involved, you might still have to pay something towards the overall cost.

If you have an issue with health care provision, contact your nearest Irish centre, which will be able to give you information on the best options available to you.

# Taxation

In most states, you will be taxed more than one form of income tax: every employee is liable for federal income tax, and some states also have state income tax.

Additionally, a number of cities and counties tax locally as well. If you work as a regular employee, all your estimated federal and local taxes are deducted from your salary, just like PAYE.

The agency responsible for the collection of taxes is the Internal Revenue Service (IRS). The tax year runs from 1 January to 31 December, and you must file a tax return every year before 15 April; this return informs the government of how much you earned and how much you were taxed.

Federal tax rates are divided into six bands: the lowest band has a rate of 10 percent, and the highest is 35 percent.

State income tax is payable in forty-one states; the rates range from 1 to 10 percent, depending on which state you live in and how much you earn. Alaska, Florida, Nevada, South Dakota, Texas, Washington and Wyoming impose no income tax.

# Employment

Your social security number is required by law in order for you to work. It is issued only to those who have a valid work or residency visa stamped on their passport.

You may need to have your qualifications evaluated in order to have them understood and recognised by educational institutions, employers, licensing and certi-fication boards in the USA. However, no US government agency evaluates qualifications. Rather, you will have to have your qualifications evaluated by universities and private organisations. When applying for work, you will be asked to submit a résumé (Curriculum Vitae or CV).

## Banking and finance

American banking institutions are either commercial or savings banks, or savings and loan associations. There are also credit unions, similar to Irish credit unions.

The two main types of account offered are checking (the equivalent of a current account) and savings. Check-ing accounts come with chequebooks and ATM and debit cards. However, instant access to savings accounts is more limited.

To open an account, take your Green Card, driver's li-cence and deposit to the bank of your choice. Some banks may also require proof of residence and your SSN. If you have not received your social security number, you can show the receipt of your application.

If you are taking a large amount of money with you, bear in mind that it can take some weeks before a bank draft is cleared, so make sure that you have access to funds to cover expenses in the meantime.

You may be able to open some kind of account upon visa approval and before you arrive, enabling you to transfer money electronically from your Irish account to your US bank.

Getting credit can be difficult in these challenging times, and emigrants usually find it more difficult than most because they have no credit rating in the country they move to. It can help to build a positive credit rating by arranging credit with local businesses and stores, and then paying your bills on time.

Even so, it may take nine to twelve months to acquire a credit rating in the USA, after which you can apply for a credit card. You may want to consider using your Irish credit card in the meantime.

# Accommodation

## Renting

Deposit costs for accommodation can be very large, ranging from $1,000 up to $3,000, depending on the area and what is required. Some landlords request the first month's rent, the last month's rent and another month's rent as a deposit in advance. Be aware that most accommodation will not have furnishing, so read your rental agreement carefully, and confirm whether your rent includes utilities such as heating, lighting and electricity.

## Property market

From 2008, property prices settled after years of double-digit percentage increases. This may yield bargains for those who can afford to buy.

## Mortgages

Most American banks offer mortgages, but the majority of these will require information on your US tax returns and credit rating. You may find that some banks will accept an Irish credit rating for mortgage purposes.

Repayment and interest-only mortgages are available in America, with banks typically lending up to 75 percent of the value of the property over a thirty-year term.

## How to buy

The exact procedures differ from state to state, but in general you'll identify a suitable property and instruct your real-estate agent, realtor or realtist to make a verbal offer. Following agreed negotiations, the seller's lawyer will prepare a contract of sale specific to the state you are in. Your lawyer checks the deed and title.

Ensure that the contract contains all the conditions that must be met – including home inspections – before it becomes binding. The seller is obliged to disclose any defect the property might have.

The buyer must pay a 'good faith' deposit on making an offer, typically 10 percent of the full price. If the offer is accepted, the contract is signed by both parties and becomes binding. The relevant documents are then filed at a public recording office.

## Fees and taxes

Real estate broker's fees are around 6 percent and are usually paid by the seller, not the buyer.

Title search and insurance costs are around 0.5 percent to 1 percent of the purchase price.

Legal costs should amount to no more than 1 percent, and the fee for recording is set at a maximum of 0.5 percent.

## Property taxes

Your property will be levied for state and local taxes, usually in order to fund schools and other services. Water rates are also often included in property taxes.

The value of your property will be assessed, and you will be charged a certain percentage of every $1,000 of that value. The tax charged depends on the size of the property and the state you live in, and can range from a few hundred to several thousand dollars.

# Utilities

ELECTRICITY AND GAS  Choice of service may be limited depending on where you live. You are likely to find that one company has a local monopoly, offering both electricity and gas. Notify them that you need supply at least a week in advance. To open an account in your name, you'll need proof of address, a deposit and your social security card. If you have yet to receive a social security card, your passport may suffice.

Electricity and gas is usually billed monthly and measured by meter readings. Your first bill will probably be higher than subsequent ones as it includes a connection fee.

In Ireland, energy bills are usually higher in the winter, particularly for light and heat. Most buildings in America have air-conditioning, especially for the hot summer months, and electricity costs during this season can be quite high as a result.

TELEPHONE  There is a choice of several telecoms companies in most locations, with a number of tariffs on offer. International call cards provide a cheap way of keeping in contact with friends and family in Ireland.

To set up a landline account, you'll need your social security number, among other documents. Your bill will arrive monthly.

TELEVISION  Several channels are available free of charge, but cable and satellite services must be paid for. There is no TV licence in America.

# Education

Each state is responsible for its own education system, paid for by local taxation. Private schooling is also available in many areas.

In most states, compulsory education starts at the age of five and lasts until the age of sixteen. The school year begins in August or September and ends in May or June. Your child might be tested to determine what class (or grade) they should be in.

## Driving

Driving licence laws differ state by state. In some cases, your Irish licence can be exchanged, and in others up to ninety days is given to obtain the relevant state licence.

You may not necessarily have to do a practical test, but may well have to sit a written test. In some states, it is necessary to sit both the practical and written tests.

You can check the exact requirements with the Department of Motor Vehicles, Department of Transportation, Motor Vehicle Administration, or Department of Public Safety in the state you're moving to.

## Useful websites

Official DV Lottery Website: *www.dvlottery.state.gov*

General US government: *www.usa.gov*

General US information website: *www.info.gov*

US Embassy, Dublin: *http://dublin.usembassy.gov/*

US Immigration: *www.uscis.gov/portal/site/uscis*

US Social Security Number: *www.ssa.gov*

Coalition of Irish Immigration Centres: *www.ciic-usa.org*

# 9

# Destination Australia

Australia's warm, sunny climate offers an abundance of opportunities for people to enjoy an outdoors lifestyle. With Irish-level salaries, a low population density, a pleasing mix of multicultural cities and natural beaches and rainforests, more and more Irish people are choosing to live and work Down Under.

## Immigration

The Department of Immigration and Citizenship (DIAC) oversees Australia's immigration programme. Visas leading to permanent residence are available in three different streams: skilled, business and family.

General information about immigration and citizenship, as well as publications, application forms and guides, are available online at the Department of Immigration's website, *www.immi.gov.au.*

If you have a query about the visa options and would like to speak to an Australian official, you can contact the Australian High Commission in London. (The Australian High Commission in Dublin does not provide an immigration service.)

## Skilled stream visas

The skilled visa stream and its many subclasses dominate the immigration programme. To qualify for one of the visas available in the skilled stream, you must:

Be under forty-five years of age

Have good English-language skills

Be skilled in your nominated occupation from the Skilled Occupation List (SOL)

Have work experience in an occupation on the SOL

Have your skills and qualifications assessed by the relevant authority (either Trades Recognition Australia or VETASSESS).

There are three key important sections within the Skilled stream:

SKILLED-INDEPENDENT VISA  This is a permanent residence visa which is designed for people who want to travel to Australia and find their own employment. The visa has a pass mark of 120 points, leads directly to permanent residence, and enables you to settle anywhere in Australia. If you score between 100 and 120 points, your application will be placed in reserve for two years. You must have your skills assessed for your occupation by the relevant Australian Authority before you can apply for this visa. You will also need to find out if the occupation you have nominated requires you to be registered or licensed, or to be a member of a professional or industrial organisation. It can take up to twelve to eighteen months for a Skilled–Independent visa application to be processed.

SKILLED-SPONSORSHIP VISA  This has a lower pass mark, of 100 points, but requires sponsorship from a relative in Australia or a state government (assuming that you have an occupation that is on the state's 'high demand' occupation list). It also requires that you live in a particular state for a certain period of time (usually two to three years) before qualifying for permanent residence. If you score between 80 and 100 points, your application will be placed in a reserve pool. If you score less than 80 points, your application will be refused.

REGIONAL-SPONSORED VISA This is similar to the Skilled-Sponsorship visa, but the applicant must reside in a designated area of the country, where employers are unable to fill skilled positions from the local labour market. The visa is initially granted on a temporary basis but can lead to permanent residence.

On submitting an application, you will be given access to the Skill Matching Database, which can help you find a job before you arrive in Australia. The database matches skilled people who have applied to migrate with skilled vacancies or listed skill shortages in Australia. It is accessed by both employers and State/Territory governments, who may then nominate a person for migration. Although this database can help you find a job before you arrive in Australia, it does not guarantee that your visa application will be approved.

### Family stream visas

Australia's family visas provide a range of options enabling spouses, prospective spouses, partners, parents, dependent children, aged dependent relatives and remaining relatives to join their sponsoring relative.

### Other visa options

There are a range of business visas allowing temporary employment in Australia, some of which can provide an opportunity for permanent residence.

Whichever visa you apply for, you'll have to pay a non-refundable processing fee, usually between €100 and €300. The cost of the visa itself ranges from a few hundred euro for a temporary visa to several thousand euro for a permanent visa. Visa charges increased on 1 July 2009, and a full list of charges is available at *www.immi.gov.au/immigration.*

## Health check requirements

Whichever visa you apply for, there are health-check and character-check requirements.

The health check may also be required of any dependant family members (including children), whether or not they are emigrating with you.

As your application is processed, an immigration case worker will notify you if you need to be examined. The case worker will nominate a panel doctor and/or radiologist. Following your examination, the doctor will send his report to the Australian immigration officials, and subsequently a Medical Officer of the Commonwealth (MOC) will examine the report and inform the department with an opinion on whether or not you meet the health requirements for your visa application.

Additionally, all visas require proof that you are of good character.

Your application may fail on the character requirement if you have a criminal record or if it is considered that there is a risk that you will be involved in crime in Australia.

You may also be asked to provide a Garda clearance certificate.

# Health care

As soon as you register with the Australian social security system, you will be entitled to family tax benefits, child care benefits and Medicare cover – one of the most highly regarded social health care systems in the world.

The Australian government recommends that you enrol in Medicare seven to ten days after your arrival. You can do this simply by taking your passport and visa to the nearest Medicare office. Further information is available on the Department of Health and Ageing's website, *www.health.gov.au.*

Although Medicare provides universal access to free or low-cost public medical, optometric and hospital care and assistance with doctors' fees, it does not cover prescriptions or ambulance charges. Also, if you receive hospital treatment, you will have to pay for accommodation, nursing and the cost of medicines.

Under Medicare, you will also be free to choose private health services. There are a range of health insurers and different types of health cover on offer. The Australian government encourages this by providing a rebate of up to 30 percent of the cost of lifetime health cover.

Medicare is financed from general taxation. Your contribution to the health care system is based on your income and is made through taxes and the Medicare levy.

To be eligible for a state pension, you must be a permanent resident for ten years.

## Taxation

You will need a tax file number (TFN) to file a return and to claim social security benefits. A TFN is available from your local Australian Tax office. You can also request an application by telephone or apply via the Australian Taxation Office website, *www.ato.gov.au.*

If you are attending the office in person, you will need to provide original documents proving your identity: passport, original birth certificate, proof of where you are staying and/or proof of your immigration status in Australia.

It is important to get your TFN as soon as possible after you arrive in Australia to ensure that you aren't automatically taxed at the highest rate, as you would be with an emergency tax code in Ireland.

Income tax is deducted by employers at source (similar to PAYE, but called 'Pay As You Go') in Australia but is paid in arrears by the self-employed.

However, anyone who earns over A$6,000 in an Australian tax year (1 July to 30 June) must file a tax return. Most people employ an accountant to do this for them.

There are four tax bands above this threshold: 15, 30, 40 and 45 percent.

## Employment

You may already have a job lined up before you leave, depending on the type of visa you're going for.

If you're looking for work in Australia, register with Centrelink for help in finding a job. Once you are registered, you can be referred to Job Network, which consists of private, community and government organisations that help people find employment.

## Banking and finance

The Australian equivalent of a current account is a cheque (or transaction) account. As in Ireland, a savings account offers higher interest but more limited access to your money. Most people have a savings account for long-term saving as well as a current account for easy access to funds. The Australian Bankers' Association is the Australian banking ombudsman, so choose a bank that is a member of this organisation.

A cheque or transaction account usually includes an

Electronic Funds Transfer at Point Of Sale card, which is essentially a debit card you can use to pay for goods and services.

While cheques are not widely used, credit cards and debit cards are commonplace.

You can open a bank account using only your passport as ID during the first six weeks after arrival. After six weeks, you will need additional identification to open an account, and you may have difficulty opening an account if you do not have all the necessary documents.

Australian post offices also now offer banking services.

# Accommodation

## Renting

Rental arrangements are usually made with a real-estate agent or directly with private landlords. They will usually ask you to sign a lease (typically for six to twelve months), but don't sign until you are happy with the terms and conditions, because the document becomes legally binding upon your signature.

A rental deposit (sometimes called a bond) of four weeks' rent is usually requested, and this will be refunded when you leave the accommodation as you found it. You also typically have to pay two to four weeks' rent in advance.

## Mortgages

Healthy competition in Australia ensures a wide range of lenders and mortgages, with plenty of brokers to provide advice.

The typical term of a mortgage is twenty-five years, but you could qualify for a thirty-year mortgage with six months of employment in Australia under your belt.

Housing loan insurance is payable when the mortgage is more than 80 percent of the value of the property.

If you are buying a home for the first time in Australia, you may be eligible for a Commonwealth First Home Buyers Grant. Contact your local council office for more information.

## How to buy

If an offer is made and accepted, the estate agent prepares a contract of sale with a specific settlement date, and the contract is then signed by both parties.

Before the settlement date, all surveys, conveyancing and financial aspects are undertaken. In some cases, lenders provide property conveyance as a free service to borrowers. If not, you will most likely have to employ a solicitor or conveyencing specialist to do the conveyencing for you.

## Fees and taxes

Stamp duty is paid on a scale from 1.25 to 6.75 percent, based on the value of the property.

Registration fees range from 0.01 to 0.6 percent, depending on the location fees relating to the property.

Legal fees range from approximately A$1,000 to A$2,000, depending on which state you are buying property in.

Conveyancing fees are not fixed by law and typically range from 0.5 to 2 percent.

Government taxes, termite and pest inspections, and surveys can also increase the cost of buying property.

## Property taxes

Council rates are determined by the value of the property, and also by each state or territory's own tax rates. At an average of A$2,000 per year for a typical family property, the quarterly fees cover local services such as maintenance of pathways and roads, and refuse collection.

Land tax ranges from 0.6 to 1.7 percent and is payable across Australia, apart from in the Northern Territory.

# Utilities

ELECTRICITY AND GAS  These are provided by regional state or territory providers and are paid for on a quarterly basis. You'll need to contact the supplier to get connected or transfer the supply into your name, and in most cases a charge will apply. Before signing a contract, ensure that you know what is expected of you. For example, the utility company may want you to sign a contract for up to three years, even if you are staying in temporary accommodation.

SOLAR POWER  Although expensive to install, this is becoming increasingly popular.

WATER  Water usage is metered. There is also an annual charge for water services, as there is for sewerage.

TELEPHONE  A connection fee and deposit will be required to connect a phone line to your home; this can be arranged by any local provider. A range of tariffs are available.

TELEVISION  There is no licence fee in Australia, with several free channels and a range of paid-for cable and satellite services on offer.

# Education

Although each individual state and territory is responsible for its own education system, full-time education up to the age of fifteen is compulsory across Australia. Many students stay on at school until they have finished Year 12, at age seventeen or eighteen. School terms run from late January or early February to December.

While state schools are usually free, about one-third of Australian children attend a private – or 'independent' – school, where fees are several thousand dollars a year but academic achievement is usually higher. Many parents opt to transfer their children from a state school to a private school when secondary education begins.

Vocational training is available at Technical and Further Education (TAFE) institutions. TAFEs provide both practical and career-oriented training and accommodate a mix of study and work.

An interesting aspect of the state education system is correspondence schools for Australian children who live in remote areas of the Australian Outback. In fact, home education is a legal option for the schooling of children in all states of Australia, with the parents taking responsibility for guiding their children through a course of study.

# Driving

You can use your Irish licence for the first three months in Australia, but if you exchange your Irish driving licence for an Australian one during this time, you won't have to do a test. After three months, you'll need a licence issued by the state or territory where you live. This requires an eyesight test and a fee. You may also be required to pass a knowledge test and a practical driving test. If you are a car-owner, it is compulsory to have third-party insurance.

# Useful contacts

Australian government Immigration Department: *www.immi.gov.au*

Australian government services: *www.australia.gov.au*

Australian Embassy Ireland: *www.irelandembassy.gov.au/dub/about/htm*

EMPLOYMENT

*www.seek.com.au*
*http://mycareer.com.au*
*https://jobsearch.gov.au*

ACCOMMODATION

*www.yha.com.au*
*www.domain.com.au*
*www.rentalproperty.com.au*

# 10

# Destination New Zealand

With its mountainous backdrop and stunning coastline, sparsely populated New Zealand is a popular choice for Irish people looking for more space and time in which to enjoy life.

## Immigration

The qualifying process for visas is overseen by Immigration New Zealand (INZ).

With many native young workers choosing to travel and live abroad, the New Zealand economy is in need of suitable skilled workers from overseas to help sustain its growth.

Therefore, of the four categories that make up New Zealand's immigration system – Skilled Migrant, Work to Residence, Family, and Business – the authorities place most emphasis on the first.

### Skilled Migrant category (SMC)

This points-based system is only open to those aged twenty to fifty-five. Selection is based on a ranking system taking into account qualifications, work experience, employment, family connections and age. The maximum score is 240, but those scoring 100 points or more in the four factors outlined can lodge an 'expression of interest.' Every two weeks, INZ picks the highest-scoring applicant from this pool and invites them to make a full application.

You can make a preliminary check to see if you meet eligibility criteria at *www.immigration.govt.nz.*

## Work to Residence category

This option allows people with qualifications in a highly specialised occupation, an occupation that is in high demand, or exceptional talents in sport or the arts, to work temporarily in New Zealand as a step towards gaining permanent residence. After two years, you can apply for permanent residence.

## Family category

This enables those with a family member who is already a New Zealand citizen or resident to move to the country. Your relationship to this person must be one of the following: conjugal partner (including same-sex partners), dependent child, parent, brother or sister, or adult child.

## Business category

New Zealand offers several temporary options: the Working Holiday Visa Scheme, the Student Visa Permit and the Work Permit.

Those looking to set up a business in New Zealand should investigate the Investor and Entrepreneur categories. Although both routes offer permanent residence, the applicant must make a substantial investment in New Zealand, sometimes in the region of NZ$2.5 million.

Processing and application fees apply to all of the above visas, and, as with neighbouring Australia, you will need medical and Garda certificates to prove that you have a clean bill of health and are of good character.

# Health care and social security

Permanent residents of New Zealand are not required to make social security payments, but you must contribute to the Accident Compensation Corporation. If you have an accident, whether at work, playing sports, at home, or in a road traffic incident, compensation is administered by the ACC. If you are working, or self-employed, a small percentage of your earnings will be deducted and paid into the ACC scheme. The self-employed have the option of contributing to a private scheme instead.

You and your partner and dependants, if applicable, are automatically entitled to state health care. Hospital treatment is free, but you must pay a charge for each outpatient consultation or treatment.

The New Zealand administration offers a full range of social security cover, such as sickness, maternity and family benefits. However, you should be aware that unemployment benefit is only available to permanent residents who have worked in the country for two years. In addition, ten years of employment are usually necessary before you qualify for a state pension.

# Taxation

You'll also need an Inland Revenue Department (IRD) number to start a job. In order to get an IRD number, visit a local IRD office with your passport and complete the relevant form for each member of the family.

The IRD number is also used to track your tax payments. Only three tax bands exist in New Zealand, and employers usually deduct tax from your salary at source.

# Employment

Immigration New Zealand regularly updates their essential-skills-in-demand lists with the latest vacancies and openings.

There are two lists: the Long Term Skill Shortage List and the Immediate Skill Shortage List. While the former is related to both temporary work policy and residence policy, the latter affords no direct link to residence.

If you meet the requirements on the list and the visa requirements, INZ will accept that no New Zealanders are available for the position.

You can search either list on its own, or you can search occupation keywords of both simultaneously at *www.immigration.govt.nz.*

# Banking and finance

Registered banks, credit unions and building societies offer banking services. Current accounts typically come with a chequebook and a debit card.

You'll need photo identification and proof of your permanent address in order to open an account. However, you should be able to find a bank that will allow you to open an account before you leave Ireland. This is an advantageous move: if you open an account after you become a permanent resident of New Zealand, you'll need an IRD number (similar to the Irish PPS number). If you don't have this, or open an account while waiting for your IRD number to be issued, the higher rate of Resident Withholding Tax – equivalent to emergency tax in Ireland – will be deducted for the interest accrued in your account.

# Accommodation

## Property market

A stand-alone wooden building is the typical New Zealand residential property. While newer houses are insulated, older houses may have minimal insulation. With a year-round climate that is generally warm, central heating and double glazing are not common.

## Mortgages

You can shop around for the best mortgage via banks, brokers and loan companies. While lenders will typically offer a maximum mortgage of 95 percent of the property's value, they tend not to permit repayments above 30 percent of your net income. The standard mortgage term is twenty-five years. Lenders charge a fee of around 1 percent.

## How to buy

Property is usually purchased with the assistance of a real-estate agent. The first stage is to make a formal offer (which in New Zealand is usually no more than 5 to 10 percent below the asking price), and is conditional upon such things as mortgage approval.

A 10 percent deposit is required on acceptance of the offer. This is followed by the signing and agreement of a contract specifying the settlement date. A real-estate agent can provide a legally binding contract.

If you pull out of the deal at this stage for a reason not covered by a specific clause, you will lose your deposit.

On average, the entire process takes about a month, but it can take as little as a week.

## Fees and taxes

The cost of purchasing (not including the mortgage) is comparatively low in New Zealand.

Registration fees for resale properties are fixed, ranging from NZ$20 to NZ$110.

Lawyer's fees range from NZ$600 to NZ$2,000.

Real-estate agent's fees, usually at around 4 percent, are typically paid by the seller. The seller often pays for marketing the property too.

## Property taxes

Everyone who owns a home must pay taxes to the district and regional councils, with the charges covering refuse collection, street lighting, water and sewerage.

Each property is assessed annually by the local government and given a 'Qualitative Value' on the basis of what the inspector thinks the property and land is worth. This value is used in determining the rates.

Auckland residents pay separate water rates and face a higher overall bill.

# Utilities

ELECTRICITY AND GAS  Power supply is privatised in New Zealand, so you'll need to contact the local company to arrange connection. Billing for all utilities is usually on a bi-monthly basis.

There is no mains gas supply on the South Island. Instead, canisters of liquid petroleum gas and gas bottles are widely used in households.

WATER  This is supplied by the local council. In some rural areas, properties have their own water tanks and septic tanks.

TELEPHONE The telecommunications market is quite competitive in New Zealand, affording a range of providers and tariffs. Proof of identity and address are needed to arrange landline connection. A line rental fee will be incurred, and there will also be a specific charge for the package you choose.

TELEVISION No licence fee applies; there are six free-to-air terrestrial stations, and numerous pay-for cable and satellite channels available.

## Education

Full-time education is compulsory between the ages of six and sixteen, although many parents enrol their children in school when they turn five. The school year starts in February and runs until November or December.

State schools are free, and mostly co-educational. Higher-education options include universities and employer-assisted apprenticeships.

## Driving

You can drive for up to a year with an Irish driving licence. Before the twelve months are up, you should apply for a New Zealand driving licence; this includes a theory test.

# Useful websites

Official New Zealand Government Immigration website: *www.immigration.govt.nz*

New Zealand Government Services: *www.govt.nz*

New Zealand Yellow Pages: *www.yellowpages.co.nz*

EMPLOYMENT

*www.seek.co.nz*
*http://www.wowjobs.co.nz*
*http://jobs.nzherald.co.nz*
*www.jobs.govt.nz*

ACCOMMODATION

*http://www.homeads.co.nz.*
*www.therentshop.co.nz*
*www.realestate.co.nz/rental*

# 11

## Destination Canada

The second-biggest country in the world, comprising a vast array of landscapes and cityscapes, Canada provides plenty of scope for Irish people looking for a better quality of life.

## Immigration

Each year, a quarter of a million people worldwide are granted permanent residence by Canada's federal immigration system, Citizenship and Immigration Canada (see the website *www.cic.gc.ca*). There are three streams for permanent residence visas:

Economic Class (skilled workers, business immigrants, provincial nominees and live-in caregivers)

Family Class (spouses and partners, children, parents and grandparents of the sponsors)

Protected Persons (refugees and those admitted on humanitarian grounds)

Skilled workers are selected for their ability to establish themselves successfully in Canada and contribute to the Canadian economy. Applicants for the Skilled Worker visa are assessed through a points-based selection grid. The grid is divided into six selection factors comprising education, language, work experience, age, arranged employment and adaptability. Points are awarded in each category, depending on experience and qualifications. (The current pass mark is 67.) Successful applicants can become permanent residents of Canada.

Perhaps the most challenging aspect of the Skilled Worker visa is the processing time, which averages forty-four to forty-eight months. However, there are two ways to reduce this waiting time considerably.

One is the Employer Sponsored Visa option, whereby you secure an Arranged Employment Offer from a Canadian employer. This is a route that senior managers and executives frequently use. With some exceptions, vacancies will need to be 'validated' by the Canadian Human Resource Centre. This is to ensure that there are no Canadians or permanent residents who can fill the vacancy before you start the process of applying for the Employer Sponsored Visa.

Another fast track to residence is the Provincial Nominee Programme. Many provinces play a direct role in selecting immigrants who wish to settle in that province. In order to apply, you'll have to contact directly the province where you wish to settle. The authorities will then consider your application based on their immigration needs and your genuine intention to settle there. After a province has nominated you, they will send you a Certificate of Provincial Nomination, and you can then make a separate application to Citizenship and Immigration Canada for permanent residence. The CIC will then assess your application to ensure that it conforms to Canadian immigration regulations.

The government of Quebec administers its own system, which leans heavily towards Francophones. See the Québec government website for information on emigrating to Québec, at *www.gouv.qc.ca*.

With both the Employer Sponsored Visa option and the Provincial Nominee Programme, processing times are less than a year, with resulting permanent residence granted on approval.

Canada's immigration system also offers two business visas: Investor and Entrepreneur. Both visas require considerable business experience and, more importantly, a lot of money. For the Investor and Entrepreneur programmes, you must have a minimum net worth of C$800,000 (€520,000 and C$300,000 (€195,000 respectively; in addition, the former requires an investment of C$400,000 (€260,000).

CIC also offers a Self-Employed Person's visa, for those who are world-class in the fields of culture or sport, or have experience in farm management.

All Business Class applications take two years or more to process.

A range of family members, including spouses, partners and dependent children of Canadian citizens and permanent residents, can be reunited with family members in Canada through the Family Class of visas. However, the sponsoring family member must undertake to support those moving to Canada for a period of three to ten years.

The processing time for Family Class visa applications is usually under twelve months.

Study visas are also available, and in some cases can help qualification for a Skilled Worker visa.

Whichever visa option is best for you, in order to emigrate to Canada successfully, you will have to show that you are in good health and do not have any criminal convictions.

# Health care

To access Medicare, Canada's national health service, you and any family members must get a health insurance card. Medicare covers visits to family doctors, many types of surgery, hospitalisation, tests, specialist treatment and most immunisations. However, ambulance services, prescriptions, and dental and optical care are not covered.

As is the case with many official services, Medicare is administered at provincial and territorial level, with important differences to be aware of. For example, some regions require a monthly fee, while there is a three-month eligibility waiting period in British Columbia, Ontario, Quebec and New Brunswick. You should obtain temporary private health insurance coverage for the duration of any such period. If you are in work, your employer might pay your private health insurance coverage.

You will have to show your Health Insurance Card when you receive medical services, or be charged for the services if you don't have the card.

Regardless of where you move in Canada, you should apply for your health insurance card as soon as possible. Visit the provincial ministry responsible for health, with your birth certificate, passport, confirmation of permanent residence, or permanent residence card. You can also get an application form from any doctor's office, hospital or pharmacy, or directly from your Ministry of Health.

# Social security

You must have a Social Insurance Number (SIN), which is the equivalent of the Irish PPS number, in order to work in Canada and receive government benefits.

SIN applications can be made at branches of Service Canada or via the Service Canada website. There is a four- to six-week processing time for the card to be issued via the post.

Through your SIN, the Canadian government tracks your taxes, pension plan contributions, and any unemployment, child care, disability or low-income benefits paid out. You'll also need a SIN to open a bank account.

Social insurance is funded through taxation on your gross salary. In addition, a small percentage will be contributed to the state pension, the Canada Pension Plan. Residents of Quebec pay into the Quebec Pension Plan, which works in the same way.

However, with social security regulation, and indeed all forms of official legislation, you should always check the rules and regulations of the province or territory in which you live, as laws are not identical across the country. Canada has a federal system, whereby the different provinces and territories are semi-autonomous. For example, health care, education and vehicle licensing are all dealt with at provincial or territorial level. You should research separately each province or territory you are thinking of moving to.

## Taxation

All residents of Canada must file an annual income tax return, whether or not they earned anything. The Income Tax and Benefit Return informs the government of how much money you earned and how much tax you paid. Employers will deduct a percentage of your salary to cover income tax, whereas the self-employed are responsible for paying income taxes.

The deadline for completion of tax returns is 30 April.

There are four federal tax bands that apply nation-wide and deduct between 15 and 29 percent of your gross income. Provincial taxes also apply; these range from about 4 to 18 percent, depending on where you live.

## Employment

The Human Resources Centres of Canada (HRCC) are public jobs centres. In each centre, you will find specialist employment counsellors and access to job banks which list job openings across Canada. Check out *www.hrsdc.gc.ca* for more information on them.

You will also need to get your Irish credentials and qualification assessed, if you have not done so already. The website *www.credentials.gc.ca* features a 'Working in Canada' search tool that enables individuals to identify occupations in Canada for which they may be qualified, as well as the regulatory body appropriate for their needs.

However, an assessment of your qualifications does not guarantee that you will be accredited with a professional licence to practise by a regulatory body. You may have to obtain local certification to continue working in some professions or trades.

Working parents should be aware that it is illegal in Canada to leave children under the age of twelve at home by themselves.

## Banking and finance

A cheque account is the Canadian equivalent of the standard Irish current account. A Canadian cheque account comes with a debit card and allows you to write cheques, although cheque-guarantee cards do not feature in the

Canadian banking system. Most bank cards can be used to pay for goods and services; typically, banks charge a small monthly administration charge for services.

While banks can provide loans and mortgages, new arrivals face a challenge in securing credit because of their lack of credit rating and credit history. However, you can build a credit profile in Canada by getting loans and store cards, and paying off the full amount on time.

You may find it useful to keep open an Irish credit card until you have established your Canadian credit rating.

# Accommodation

## Renting

Depending on where you live, you could expect to pay $500 a month for a room and between $1,000 and $2,000 a month for an apartment or a house.

Rental costs vary greatly across Canada, with better deals available outside the large cities.

You may be asked to sign a twelve-month lease on an apartment or house you want to rent, although some properties are rented monthly. The landlord or letting agent will probably ask for the first and last month's rent in advance as part of the lease agreement. You may also be asked to pay a security deposit to secure the property for your use, but be aware that in some provinces it is illegal for a landlord to ask for a security deposit or a damage deposit. Note also that the precise rental laws differ from province to province.

## Property market

In common with many property markets around the world, house prices in Canada began to level out from 2007 onwards.

## Mortgages

Mortgages in Canada are defined in two categories: open mortgages, which you can repay without penalty, and closed mortgages, which are more restrictive. Financial regulations prohibit Canadian lenders from lending more than 75 percent of the market vale of a property in question, while banks rarely lend more than 65 percent to newcomers.

However, you should investigate whether you are eligible for government-backed mortgage insurance run by the Canada Mortgage and Housing Corporation, which can increase the mortgage availability to 90 to 95 percent of the value of the property. The scheme also allows you to buy a home with a smaller down payment.

Few lenders will approve a mortgage that requires more than 30 percent of your gross monthly income to repay. In contrast, lenders can prove flexible in negotiating the terms of the mortgage. While twenty-five years is standard, some lenders will agree to forty-year terms.

Note that it can sometimes take a lender as long as ninety days to approve a mortgage.

## How to buy

Most homes in Canada are sold through real-estate agents, although some owners do it themselves. Once you have found a property you like, your real-estate broker will prepare an offer to purchase, possibly in conjunction with a lawyer.

With price agreement between buyer and seller, a 10 percent deposit is due to the seller. Upon payment, a copy of the signed agreement is examined by a lawyer for any conditions placed on the sale. Any such conditions must be completed by the specified closing date.

Following this, legal checks on the property title are

made. A legal document is drawn up stating the terms of the deal, including asking price, deposit paid, and amount outstanding. A certified cheque for the outstanding amount is then paid to the seller.

Finally, the lawyer registers the home in the buyer's name and provides the buyer with a deed.

## Fees and taxes

Real-estate agents/realtors in general charge 7 percent on the first C$100,000 of the sale and 3 percent on the remainder. In most cases, the seller usually pays the agent's fee. However, where there is both a selling and a buying agent involved, the fee may be divided between the seller and buyer.

There is a minimum charge of C$500 for legal fees.

Land/property/purchase transfer tax ranges from 0.5 to 2 percent, depending on the price of the property.

New property and extensively renovated resale property have a Goods and Service tax of 6 percent. (Partial rebates are possible in some cases.)

An Estoppel certificate is required for those buying an apartment (Quebec excluded); this costs around C$100.

Other charges may apply for a property appraisal, home inspection and survey, if applicable.

## Property taxes

Taxes are levied against each C$100,000 of a property's value to fund municipal charges such as refuse collection and the emergency services. The rates vary between each province.

# Utilities

ELECTRICITY, GAS AND OIL In any given area, one or two main companies will provide utility services. The majority of Canadian homes are heated by gas or oil, with some heated by hydro (electricity).

Your passport, property deeds or proof of address, as well as a deposit, will be required for the set-up procedure. The company in question will read the meter as part of the process, and it is likely that a charge will be incurred.

WATER Depending on where you live, water rates are either billed by the local government administration or included in your property taxes.

TELEPHONE A local telephone company will be able to install a landline for you and arrange connection, which will require a connection charge and, in some cases, a deposit. Most monthly tariff options cover line rental and local calls. Long-distance and overseas calls are usually not covered by your monthly fee and can be quite expensive. International phone cards present a highly competitive alternative.

TELEVISION Four nationwide channels are available for free. No TV licence fee applies. Cable and satellite services are available on subscription.

# Education

Each province is responsible for its own education system. Note that in Francophone Quebec and bilingual New Brunswick, most classes are taught in French, with immersion classes for those who need to ramp up their French skills in a hurry.

Public education is free and funded through taxation. Most children go to public schools. In addition, there are a number of Catholic schools and private schools. The choice available is usually based on where you live.

Most children start going to school when they are four or five. By law, children must attend school until the age of fifteen or sixteen, again depending on where they live.

Various opportunities exist for education beyond secondary school, including community colleges, universities and professional schools.

# Driving

Licences are issued by each province or territory, and the law on driving with an Irish licence varies from province to province. In general, your Irish licence will be valid for ninety days after arrival; at this point, you will need to exchange your licence or take a Canadian driving test.

The authorities in British Columbia, Prince Edward Island, Nova Scotia, Newfoundland and Labrador, as well as Canada's three territories, require you to take a test within three months of arrival.

# Useful websites

Official Canadian Government Immigration website: *www.cic.gc.ca*

EMPLOYMENT

*www.monster.ca*
*www.jobs-emplois.gc.ca*
*www.workopolis.com*
*www.canadajobs.com*
*www.jobs.ca*
*www.allstarjobs.ca*
*www.careerjet.ca*

# ACCOMMODATION

*www.ontarioaccommodation.com*
*www.uniqueaccommodations.com*
*www.thestar.com/classifieds*
*www.hihostels.ca/en*
*www.backpackers.ca*
*www.www.gottarent.com*

*www.sublet.com*
*www.pmrentals.com*
*www.relocatecanada.com*

# 12

# Destination Continental Europe

## SPAIN

Spain, with its sandy Mediterranean coast, vibrant urban centres, affordable cost of living and enticing culture, has much to offer. But Irish emigrants to Spain probably have one thing on their mind: the fact that the climate is warm year-round.

## Immigration

Officially, Spanish residency cards are not necessary for EU nationals, who may live and work in Spain just using their passports. In practice, though, having a residency permit will help expedite general bureaucratic matters. You can apply for a residency permit at a national police station that has an immigration office.

Prior to applying for a residence permit, you will need your local council offices to provide documentation (known as a *certificado de empadronamiento*, or *padrón*) that proves you live in Spain. To do this, you will have to present your passport and utility bills (with your Spanish address) to the local authority.

When they provide you with the documentation, take it to the national police station with:

The original and a copy of completed and signed application forms

Three colour passport photos

Your passport and a copy of your personal details

Some form of proof of address (title deeds to your property, rental contract, or utility bills)

Proof that you have paid the permit fees, which must be paid via a bank

A certificate of health from any Spanish doctor

A certificate of good conduct from the Gardaí

A certificate related to your marital status (if you are married), translated into Spanish.

If moving with your family, they will also be required to show their passports and photographs.

If you are retired, you will be asked to prove you have sufficient means to get by, as well as evidence of your health cover, be it a private health insurance scheme or entitlement to the Spanish public health system.

An application for a residence permit may take several weeks to complete, but you will be given a temporary permit to use while you wait for the permanent documents to arrive.

The Spanish equivalent of your Irish PPS number, known as a foreigner's identification number or Número de Identificación de Extranjero (NIE), will be issued at this time, if you have not already received it. The NIE is necessary for purchasing property, opening a bank account and arranging credit terms.

# Health care and social security

If you live and work in Spain, you are obliged to pay into the Spanish social security (Seguridad Social) system. The contributions you have to pay are calculated as a percentage of your taxable income.

In some cases, your employer will register your payments for you. If they do not, the onus is on you to register with the local social security office, for which you need to bring your passport, proof of residence, birth certificate, and marriage certificate, if applicable. You will then receive a health card, which you will need to present to your local health centre in order to register there.

The range of care covered by the national health system includes general and specialist medical care, hospitalisation, subsidised medicines and basic dental work.

# Taxation

The Spanish tax year runs from 1 January to 31 December. As a resident, it is your responsibility to file an annual tax return with the Agencia Tributaria (tax office). Income tax (*Impuesto sobre la Renta de las Personas Fisicas*, or IRPF), is divided into four bands, ranging (in total with combined national and regional taxation) from 24 to 43 percent of your annual income.

Savings and dividends are taxed at a single flat rate of 18 percent.

# Banking and finance

Most Spanish banks offer an ATM card for use at cash points. Clearing banks (*bancos*) usually offer chequebooks, while savings banks (*cajas de ahorras*) typically record your transactions in a savings book (*libreta de ahorras*). Both savings and current accounts incur an annual administration charge.

# Property market

After a decade or so of sustained boom in the Spanish property market, fuelled by overseas buyers, property prices began to stall, and in some areas dropped considerably, from late 2007.

Madrid and Barcelona, as well as areas particularly popular with British tourists, such as the Balearic Islands and the province of Malaga, have among the highest property prices.

### Mortgages

Most Spanish banks offer repayment mortgages. The maximum lending amount is usually around 80 percent of the property value, with fifteen years being the typical term of repayment.

### How to buy

Several types of contractual agreements with the seller exist, such as a reservation contract, deposit agreement, and option-to-buy agreement. Which is used depends on the working customs of the region in which you hope to buy.

Ideally, you should arrange a properly negotiated bilateral private sale agreement, which is the most secure type of contract between buyer and seller. Such a contract specifies the agreed price, date and conditions under which the transaction will take place. This is a binding contract, and should be checked by a lawyer. You should also direct the lawyer to ensure that escape clauses are in place.

A deposit of 10 percent is generally payable when the contract is signed.

If you are buying a property that is part of a complex, you will more than likely be joining a community of owners who must share the costs of maintaining the swimming pools, gardens and communal spaces.

The deed of sale legally transfers the property into your ownership. This document must be signed in the presence of a notary. The notary is also responsible for recording your ownership in the property register and the tax register.

## Fees and taxes

The fees for an estate agent in Spain range from 6 to 10 percent of the property's value. Clarify with your agent who pays these fees and how much should be paid.

VAT, at 7 to 9 percent, is payable on new-builds and properties sold on completion.

Property transfer tax is charged at 6 to 7 percent on re-sale properties (excluding those sold before completion)

Stamp duty of 0.5 to 1 percent is payable on properties subject to VAT.

Notary fees are approximately 0.5 percent. Legal fees are typically 1 to 1.5 percent.

## Property taxes

Whoever is resident in the property on 1 January must pay property tax to the local council at rates ranging from 0.3 to 1.7 percent.

Refuge and drainage tax can range from €50 to €450 per annum.

# Utilities

ELECTRICITY  If your property is new, you will have to arrange for electricity connection through an electrician or the local energy supplier. You will need a connection certificate and a first occupation licence for this; both are available from the town hall.

If your property isn't new, make sure that you avoid paying the previous owner's bill by asking the supplier to take a special meter reading. Only sign the contract for your account once the meter reading has been taken.

Most properties in Spain are connected to the standard 220v supply. In the event that you buy or rent an older property, there is a chance that it is still wired to run on 110v. If you are planning on renovating such as a property, be aware that converting the electricity system will be costly.

GAS  Most major cities in Spain have a mains gas supply, and connection is similar to connecting to electricity.

WATER  Water usage is metered, and a monthly or quarterly standing charge will have to be paid. To register the contract in your name, you generally have to visit the local council, taking property deeds and proof of identification.

TELEPHONE  If you move into a new property, you will need a landline installed by the national company Telefónica. You can request this through one of the company's offices, or a telephone shop. There are plenty of tariffs to choose from.

TELEVISION  There is no TV licence in Spain, and both free and subscription services are available.

## Education

While the Castilian language is used in the state education system, classes may also be conducted in Catalan, Basque or Galician, depending on which part of the country you live in.

If you would prefer your children to be educated in English, and have the money to pay for it, private and international schools can be found in the bigger cities.

## Driving

In theory, an Irish driving licence will suffice in Spain. However, for greater ease of dealing with police and the authorities, it is worth exchanging it for a Spanish one.

* * *

# FRANCE

With a long history of relations between the two countries, France is a perennially popular destination for Irish people who want to immerse themselves in its distinct culture.

## Immigration

As with Spain, France no longer insists on EU nationals obtaining residency cards (*cartes de séjour*), and you can live and work in France using your EU passport. However, like Spain, it may be worth applying for a *carte de séjour*, depending on the rules in your area, as your local council may still fine those who are unable to produce the card.

You must register as a resident within three months of living in France. You can register at your local town hall, where you will be asked for your passport and proof of address.

There are two types of permit; which one you apply for depends on your status, and whether you are working and receiving an income in France (*actif*) or retired or studying (*inactif*). The documentation for *actif* residents is the 'EC all occupation' document. An application requires a valid passport and declaration of employment from the employer.

The permit for *inactif* residents is the *carte de séjour*. An application requires a valid passport, proof of medical insurance, and proof of funds for the applicant and dependent family members resident in France.

## Health care and social security

If you live and work in France, you must pay into the French social security system via a tax on your income.

If your employer doesn't register you, go to your local primary sickness insurance office, Caisse Primaire d'Assurance Maladie (CPAM), for registration. You will need your passport, French residency document, proof of residence and documents proving family relationships, where applicable. These certificates may need to be translated first.

Upon registration, you will receive a health card (*carte vitale*), which will display your name and social security number.

Under France's universal health cover system, Couverture Maladie Universelle (CMU), medical services received have to be paid for up front; the costs are later reimbursed via your health card. Up to 70 percent of medical expenses may be reimbursed.

Note that this only applies when you attend medical centres that are part of the state health care system or have an agreement with the state. If you attend a private clinic, any possible reimbursements via your health card will be much lower, and you may even find that any private medical insurance you have does not cover all private services.

Under the French social security system, you may be entitled to health care benefits, occupational benefits, family benefits and pensions. But you may need to contribute to the social security system for a certain period of time before you are eligible.

## Taxation

There are seven bands in the French income tax rate, ranging from zero to 40 percent. Rebates and exemptions are granted on gross income; this can greatly reduce your bill.

Unlike Ireland, France does not operate a PAYE system, so you'll be responsible for filing your own income tax return before the 31 May deadline.

## Banking and finance

The French post office (La Poste) offers a cheap service for everyday banking needs. Generally, French banks are categorised as commercial, co-operative or savings. If you want to apply for a loan or mortgage from a co-operative bank, you'll need to become a member and will have to buy shares in the bank.

Note that interest isn't paid on current accounts; saving accounts are available at savings, commercial and co-operative banks.

## Property market

Property prices in France have risen steadily over the past decade but, as elsewhere in Europe, have recently levelled off or fallen. However, prices haven't crashed to the same extent as in Ireland, thanks to changes to the inheritance tax system in 2007, designed to promote home-ownership.

## Mortgages

Most French banks offer mortgages – typically repayment mortgages with a term of fifteen years. Banks lend from 66 to 80 percent of the property value. However, French financial regulations prohibit banks from lending an amount in excess of 30 percent of your net disposable income to repay per month.

## How to buy

Once a price is agreed and a promise to sell has been made, the *compromise de vente* (sales agreement) commits buyer and seller to the deal, and fixes a date by which transfer of ownership must take place.

On signing the agreement, you must pay a deposit of around 10 percent. There then follows a seven-day cooling-off period, during which either party can pull out without penalty.

If you pull out after this period, you lose your 10 percent deposit, whereas if the seller reneges, they pay double.

However, your lawyer can negotiate appropriate 'get out' clauses when drawing up the sales agreement. These clauses allow you to walk away from the deal without penalty under pre-defined circumstances, such as being refused a mortgage.

## Fees and taxes

Estate agents' commission varies from 5 to 10 percent. This fee is usually paid by the seller.

VAT is 19.6 percent on a property which is less than five years old and is being sold for the first time, or on an older property that has been renovated within the last five years. Stamp duty for properties over five years old is 4.8 percent.

Mortgage registration fees for the arrangement of the loan range between 1 and 3 percent.

Notary fees are around 1 to 2 percent.

## Property taxes

Land tax, charged at rates around €100 to €300, is based on a property's theoretical rental value. This tax can be waived for two years if the property has been recently renovated.

Occupancy tax is paid by whoever is resident in the property on 1 January. Both land tax and occupancy should amount to no more than a few hundred euro.

Refuse tax may be part of the land tax or charged separately.

# Utilities

Each service provider must be contacted in order to set up a contract. You will need identification, proof of address and bank account details for direct debit options.

ELECTRICITY AND GAS  Nationalised state companies run electricity and gas services. (EDF deals with electricity; Gaz de France with gas.) Both offer a range of tariffs. Bottled gas are widely available and can also be delivered to houses that are not connected to the mains gas supply.

SOLAR POWER  Solar power has become increasingly popular in recent years, with EDF tapping into solar power for general energy production, and some individual homeowners powering their homes with their own solar panels.

WATER  Unlike gas and electricity, which is nationalised, water in France is supplied by private companies. The companies measure the supply on a metered basis, and charges vary from region to region.

REFUSE  Bin collections are managed at a local level, and local charges apply.

TELEPHONE  France Télécom can arrange the installation of a telephone line or transfer the contract into your name.

TELEVISION  A compulsory annual TV licence is usually added to your occupancy tax; it can be paid as a monthly standing order.

## Education

The French educational system is highly centralised, with the school calendar running from early September to mid-July throughout the country.

Schooling is divided into primary education (*enseignement primaire*), secondary education (*enseignement secondaire*) and higher education (*enseignement supérieur*).

Primary and secondary schools are predominantly public and are either free or have low fees. Higher education has both private and public elements.

# Driving

Although it is not obligatory to do so, it is well worth exchanging your Irish licence for a French one because some French officials don't follow the European directive allowing you to drive with your Irish licence. In addition, you'll find it easier to get insurance with a French licence. Apply for a French driving licence with your local *préfecture*.

\* \* \*

# PORTUGAL

With its warm climate and largely underdeveloped coastline, Portugal offers many attractions to the Irish emigrant.

## Immigration

No more than thirty days after the initial three months of your residency in Portugal, you must register with the local immigration service office, Serviço de Estrangiros e Fronteiras (SEF). They will grant you a registration certificate, which will remain valid for five years. When applying for the certificate, you will need a valid passport, along with a sworn declaration that you:

Work under a contract of employment or are self-employed in Portugal

Have sufficient resources for yourself and your family (if applicable).

Any family members with you are also required to apply for a registration certificate, and will need to provide a valid passport and some form of document proving the family relationship.

You will also need to apply for a tax number at the local tax office. It may take some weeks to process your application for the tax number, which is required for you to receive an income and buy a house or car, but you will be issued with a temporary number in the meantime.

## Health care and social security

Only when you have obtained your registration certificate, started work and applied for a national insurance card at your local health centre can you benefit from the Portuguese national health system, the Serviço Nacional de Saúde (SNS). Until you have a national insurance card, you will be eligible for free emergency treatment only.

Many (though not all) hospital treatments are free under the Portuguese health system. You must pay up front yourself, although you will be able to claim for 50 to 100 percent of the cost, depending on the treatment received.

To begin making social security contributions, you must contact the Regional Centre of Social Security. Between 10 and 15 percent of an employee's salary income will be deducted to cover national health insurance, with the employer topping this up to around 20 percent.

## Taxation

Portugal's tax system is similar to Ireland's in that it has a PAYE process and runs from January to December. Personal income tax, which is assessed annually, is broken down into six categories, ranging from 10.5 to 42 percent. It is up to you to submit an annual tax return for income received, and this must be filed in the first four months of the following year. There are penalties for non-compliance, so it is worth seeking professional advice.

# Banking and finance

Your passport, tax number card, residency certificate and proof of residence should be all you need to open an account. Most banks offer both current accounts and savings accounts. Interest is paid on both types, but they are both also subject to tax.

Upon opening an account, a bank card will be issued to your home address. The cards can be used with chip-and-pin machines and ATMs, and as credit cards.

Cheques, while not unheard of, are not common. This facility will have to be specifically requested, and may incur an administration charge.

# Property market

Laws enforcing strict development controls, particularly around the Algarve area, means that the Portuguese property market has been characterised by only moderate growth. In such heavily regulated locations, the rate of transactions is moderate.

### Mortgages

Mortgage fees are extremely high in Portugal – sometimes as much as 15 percent of the purchase price. Most banks offer mortgages which are based on the lender's valuation of the property, which could be less than the purchase price.

The average term on offer is fifteen years, with banks typically lending no more than 80 percent of the value of the property.

## How to buy

Both buyer and seller agree a legally binding promissory contract, outlining the conditions of sale. A deposit (typically 10 to 30 percent of the purchase price) must be paid on agreement. Any conditional clauses, such as surveys, must be fulfilled, or the contract is invalid.

The formal transfer of the property takes place at the signing of the final deed, which must be witnessed by a notary.

## Fees and taxes

Estate agent commissions range from 3 to 6 percent. The commission is usually included in the asking price.

Transfer tax is only paid on resale properties. The tax varies depending on the property price, location and planned use: 5 to 6 percent is typical. VAT of 21 percent is charged on new properties.

Conveyance fees are around 1 to 2 percent. Notary fees usually amount to no more than €200 to €250.

Stamp duty is normally no more than 1 percent.

## Property taxes

You should allow 0.2 to 0.8 percent for council taxes, which are levied at different rates according to the property's value, age and type.

# Utilities

You may be able to arrange connection with the utility companies online or by telephone. However, the company may request your presence in person at their local office. You will need to bring your passport, tax number, contact details for the previous owner, and property deeds.

ELECTRICITY    Electricdade de Portugal (*www.edp.pt*) supplies electricity, and charges at various tariffs.

GAS  There is a mains gas supply throughout most of Portugal; in other areas, bottled gas is available.

WATER  The provision of water supplies falls under the remit of your local council or government administration, with whom you will need to register.

TELEPHONE  Telecom Portugal will install your landline, but you subsequently have a number of service providers to choose between.

TELEVISION  Although there is no licence fee for terrestrial TV, you will have to pay a fee to subscribe to cable and satellite channels.

## Education

If you have children and want them to continue with their education in English, you will find most English-language and international schools in and around Lisbon and the Algarve.

## Driving

While officially your Irish licence is recognised in Portugal, in practice you will find your dealings with the authorities are much smoother if you exchange it for a Portuguese licence.

\* \* \*

# ITALY

Celebrated for its cuisine and culture, Italy has plenty to attract Irish people who are in search of a better life abroad.

## Immigration

Within three months of arrival, Irish nationals must obtain a residence certificate from the local town hall's registry office. This process will require a valid passport, proof of address, and evidence of employment or financial resources (bank statements or tax returns).

The authorities can take weeks, and in some cases months, to process your application for a residence certificate, so you should submit your application early in your stay, as it is needed for important tasks like opening a bank account.

It's not obligatory, but obtaining an EU citizen's permanent residence card may be useful for future dealings with Italian authorities. This application, called a blue kit, can be made at a post office or at your local town hall. In support of your blue-kit application, you will need:

A valid passport and four recent passport photographs

Your date of arrival in Italy and the reason for your stay

Documents proving the relationship to you of family members who have moved to Italy with you

## Health care and social security

If you are a working resident of Italy, you will need to pay Italian national insurance to fund the national insurance system.

You can register with your local health authority to obtain a health card entitling you to low-cost or free treatment. Once you are in possession of a health card, you can register with a doctor.

Hospital services are usually free, and up to 75 percent of the cost will be deducted from outpatient and dental treatments.

If you are unemployed or retired but have not reached the state pension age, you will have to prove that you have sufficient funds or alternative health insurance.

## Taxation

You will need a tax code for a range of tasks, such as to register a car, pay bills, start paid employment and register with the national health service. You can get a tax code by presenting your passport at the local tax office.

Income tax is generally deducted at source from salaried workers; the tax rate for individuals ranges from 23 to 43 percent.

Self-employed workers will need to file their own tax return and organise their own tax payments.

## Banking and finance

Italian banks are either commercial, co-operative or co-cooperative credit. Most banks offer similar debit and credit cards and cheque options as in Ireland, but banking administration charges are higher. To open an account, you may be asked for:

A valid passport or birth certificate, or both

A valid residence certificate or proof of address in Italy

Proof of income (tax return or contract)

A reference from your Irish bank.

# Property market

## Mortgages

A repayment mortgage with a term of fifteen years is the typical home loan, with the maximum loan being between 60 and 80 percent of the property cost. Financial regulations prevent banks from lending an amount that would mean that your repayments would exceed more than 30 to 33 percent of your net monthly disposable income.

## How to buy

A written offer can be made before the contract is drawn up. The written offer is binding for up to fifteen days.

The terms of the deal will be outlined in a preliminary purchase contract. On signing, you must pay a deposit; this could be up to a third of the purchase price. The standard completion date is two to three months from the signing of the contracts.

A notary must administer the deed or public sale contract, in which title to the property is officially transferred to you.

## Fees and taxes

Estate agents' commission is around 3 percent each from buyer and seller.

Registration tax ranges from zero to 10 percent, depending on whether the property is new, where it is located, and whether or not you are a first-time buyer.

Depending upon your circumstances, stamp duty/ land registry tax and mortgage tax is either a small fixed fee or 1 percent each from both buyer and seller.

VAT is 10 percent if you bought new from a developer, 4 percent if it will be your main home, and 20 percent if it is designated as 'deluxe'.

Fees for conveyancing, typically undertaken by a lawyer, are around 1 to 2 percent. Notary fees are fixed in bands by law, and usually total less than 1 percent.

### Property taxes

Council tax is charged at 4 to 6 percent of the land registry value. However, it does not include rubbish collection, for which there are separate charges.

## Utilities

If the property is new, you will probably have to pay for utility services to be connected.

Otherwise, arrange for the meters to be read before setting up the account in your name, to avoid paying the bills of previous occupants.

Water supplies are sometimes managed by local authorities, who often charge a separate tax. Contact your local town hall for connection.

ELECTRICITY AND GAS   A mains gas network stretches throughout most of Italy, with gas bottles more often used in rural areas. Enel (*www.enel.it*) is the main electricity service provider.

TELEPHONE   Telecom Italia will service your installation.

TELEVISION   An annual subscription fee is payable to the state TV company via the post office.

## Education

There are some international and English-language schools throughout Italy, but most are based around Rome.

# Driving

You can use your Irish driving licence for up to twelve months after arrival. After this, you'll need to exchange it for an Italian one.

\* \* \*

# GERMANY

Germany regularly features highly in European and international 'quality of life' surveys; a move there promises a high standard of living and a healthy work-life balance.

# Immigration

You should register with the police at the residency office of your local town hall within seven days of moving into permanent accommodation. You will need a valid passport and proof of address to register. Note that if you state that you are Christian or Jewish on the registration form, you will be liable to pay a church tax. Church tax varies from region to region but is around 8 percent of your income tax. On submitting your application, you will be issued with a registration card.

EU citizens can also apply for a certificate stating their right of residence. To do so, you'll need a valid passport, proof of health insurance, evidence of employment, proof of monthly earnings, or evidence of pension, if applicable.

# Health care and social security

If you live and work in Germany, you are obliged to contribute to the social security system. Both employed and self-employed workers are automatically enrolled in Germany's social security system, which is overseen by the Ministry for Health and Social Security. Contributions are automatically deducted from taxable income on employed workers, whereas self-employed workers must pay their own contributions.

Unless you earn in excess of approximately €50,000 per annum, you will be automatically enrolled in the state health insurance scheme.

German social security covers health care, sickness, maternity, unemployment benefits, and pensions.

# Taxation

If you plan to work, you should ask for an income tax card when you register as a resident. Your tax class will then be allotted, based on your current marital, familial and employment status.

Income tax is deducted at source by your employer for the period 1 January to 31 December. If you have no other source of income, you do not need to file an income tax return. Income tax rates range from 15 to 45 percent.

# Banking and finance

There are three main types of bank (public savings, private commercial and credit co-operatives); they all offer current and savings accounts. Cash, debit and credit cards are widely used, but an annual charge applies in many cases. Your passport, proof of registration, and proof of address are required to open an account.

# Property market

Most Germans rent their homes, with the property market typified by a lower level of home ownership than in other central European countries. Apartments, rather than houses, dominate the housing stock, although there is a choice of properties in larger urban areas. Property in Berlin costs far less than homes in most other European capitals, and if you were to buy a house in Germany today, you'll pay in or around what you would have paid a decade ago.

## Mortgages

Mortgages are based on the value assigned to a property by the bank or mortgage bank in question. Banks tend to lend no more than 60 to 70 percent of their valuation. Both fixed and variable repayment mortgages can be arranged, with thirty years typically the maximum term.

## How to buy

When you identify a suitable property, you can make an offer via your agent. A deposit will then be required; this can range from 10 to 25 percent.

A notary will check to see if there are any restrictions on the sale and use of the property. If there are no restrictions, and buyer and seller agree to the contract, the notary registers the change of ownership with the government and the transaction is officially lodged in the land register.

The notary will send a copy of the contract to the Finance Office, and the buyer must then pay property purchase tax. Upon payment, a clearance certificate will be issued by the tax office. With this, the transfer is completed.

## Fees and taxes

Estate agents' fees are generally 3 to 7 percent of the purchase price, often split between buyer and seller. Property transfer tax is 3.5 percent. Stamp duty ranges from 0.2 to 0.5 percent. Notary fees are usually 1 to 1.5 percent.

## Property taxes

Municipal services, such as water costs and refuse collection, are billed on a monthly basis.

# Utilities

ELECTRICITY Electricity services are provided by a choice of companies, supplemented by electricity brokers, who offer a range of tariffs. Whatever service and tariff you choose, have the meter read before you establish the contracts in your name, to avoid paying outstanding bills run up by the previous occupant. Proof of identity and address will be required when setting up utility accounts.

GAS Bottled gas is used in some remote areas, but on the whole gas is not widely available.

WATER: Water costs are considered incidental charges, and are billed monthly, along with bin collection.

TELEPHONE Contact a Deutsche Telekom office and complete an application form for line installation. Phone services are available from several companies.

TELEVISION An annual licence fee must be paid to the Central Office for Licensing Fees for Radio and Television. Additional cable and satellite channels cost extra.

## Education

Most schools are public. Private and international schooling is available in Germany, particularly in the larger cities.

## Driving

You can use your Irish driving licence if you wish, although as elsewhere, exchanging your Irish licence for a local one may make dealing with authorities a little easier.

\* \* \*

### USEFUL WEBSITES FOR CENTRAL EUROPE

European Citizen Action Service: *www.ecas.org*

European Commission Representation in Ireland: *http://ec.europa.eu/ireland/welcome*

European Commission: *http://ec.europa.eu/index_en.htm*

European Union Website: *http://europa.eu/index_en.htm*

European Health Insurance Card: *www.ehic.ie*

Employment related information: *www.europass.ie/europass*

EURES (Employment in Europe and general country information): *http://ec.europa.eu/eures/home.jsp*

European Business Directory: *www.europages.net*

# 13

# Destination UAE

The United Arab Emirates is composed of seven emirates: Abu Dhabi, Dubai, Sharjah, Ajman, Umm Al Qaiwain, Ras Al Khaimah and Fujairah.

The UAE has witnessed a remarkable and swift economic development, which, combined with minimal tax laws, is attracting many international workers to its building and nursing industries in particular.

## Immigration

Each Emirate has nuances within the overall UAE immigration process. However, permanent residence is generally not an option. Instead, renewable labour and residence visas for up to three years are available for workers who are under fifty years of age and are in secure employment.

Permission to employ an individual must be obtained in advance by the sponsoring employer in the UAE from the authorities concerned. The employer will require valid passport details of the prospective employee and professional and educational certificates demonstrating evidence that the candidate is right for the post.

An entry permit will be issued upon approval, enabling the candidate to enter the country for employment purposes.

You will need to take a medical test and obtain a health card. Individuals who test positive for AIDS will not be approved for a residence visa. The health card can be issued at the Ministry of Health or at a recognised private hospital.

The family of overseas workers can be sponsored also. The family visa allows you to sponsor your parents, spouse, and children under the age of eighteen. However, family visas are only possible if you earn more than Dh4,000 (€770) a month.

Another way to get into the UAE is the investor/business visa; this is issued when the applicant has a minimum of Dh70,000 (€13,500) in share capital, and is issued for an initial three-year period.

While the paperwork for work permits and residential permits is fairly straightforward, the realities of life in the UAE can be very culturally challenging for Irish people, and there are some crucial laws and customs to be aware of.

The UAE is a Muslim country in which Islamic law is enforced. Women dress in a modest way, particularly in Sharjah and Ajman, where Islamic law is rigorously enforced. Clothes cover the tops of the arms and legs, and underwear should not be visible. Public displays of affection are frowned upon, and sex outside of marriage is illegal, as is cohabitation, adultery and homosexual behaviour.

Additionally, importing narcotics and pork products is forbidden, while videos, books and magazines are subject to scrutiny and may be censored.

The consumption of alcohol is restricted but not impossible. Drink licences can be obtained by residents to consume alcohol in private homes, and alcoholic drinks are served in licensed hotels and clubs. However, it is a punishable offence to drink, or be drunk, in public. There is a zero-tolerance policy for drinking and driving, and the penalties can be severe. Drugs law are also severe: the presence of drugs in the body is counted as possession, and carries a minimum sentence of four years' imprisonment.

If you are considering a move to the UAE, it is worth familiarising yourself with the traditions of a Muslim society, in order to avoid the possibility of committing any faux pas.

## Health care and social security

You are urged to obtain comprehensive travel insurance, including medical insurance, before travelling to the UAE.

Standards of health care are considered to be generally high in the UAE, but health care currently is free only for UAE citizens, so you will also need to arrange private health cover. It is becoming more common for firms hiring overseas workers to offer private medical cover as a benefit.

Social welfare, including unemployment benefit, is only payable to UAE nationals.

In fact, there are no obligatory state or employer-contribution insurance schemes in the UAE. The gross national product, primarily based on oil, allows the Gulf states to fund the welfare of their people without needing to impose many financial obligations upon them. Nationals are automatically provided with state help, including medical care, sickness and maternity cover, child care, pensions, unemployment benefit and, in some instances, housing and disability benefits.

There are no state pension schemes for overseas workers, although certain state institutions and some international companies have corporate pension schemes.

# Taxation

The UAE is a particularly attractive destination for over-seas workers because of the almost-zero tax policy on personal taxes.

An income tax decree has been enacted by each Emirate, but in practice the enforcement of these decrees is restricted to foreign banks and oil companies, rather than individual workers. There is no individual income tax in the UAE, nor are there investment, wealth, capital gains, inheritance and gift, property or stamp duty taxes.

There are some municipal taxes charged locally, with the rate and application varying from state to state.

Generally, there is no tax on sales or VAT, but individual states may charge levies on certain products, such as alcohol and cigarettes, and on certain services, such as those provided in the hospitality industry.

There is a standard 5 percent importation duty on most imports throughout the UAE, with higher rates being applied to alcohol and tobacco.

# Employment

The building boom has slowed in recent years, but both private- and public-sector employers continue to recruit overseas workers with special skills. They often do so through overseas employment agencies, and you will find that many Irish recruitments specialists have a list of UAE opportunities. UAE jobs are also often listed in the press and in professional journals.

# Banking and finance

Many international and local banks are represented in the UAE. You can open a bank account when you arrive, although you will not be able to use all the facilities – notably chequebooks – until you have a residency visa. You will be able to get a credit card. However, cheques are particularly important in Dubai, where you will need to deposit cheques with your landlord or use a cheque to buy a car.

Usually, your employer will have a preferred bank, which should be willing to offer services such as car and housing loans and will be helpful when it comes to opening an account and administering the paperwork.

# Accommodation

## Renting

Accommodation can be expensive, and there is sometimes stiff competition in areas popular with overseas workers. Neighbourhoods are safe further away from the business hubs, but this will entail a commute. Cars and taxis are the main way of getting around, so the roads can get choked in busy times.

Unlike in Ireland, you will normally have to pay for the entire year of tenancy in advance, either with cash or cheques. In addition to the tenancy payment, if the accommodation was taken through a property agency, you have to pay a 5 percent commission to the agent.

Most landlords will demand a refundable security deposit of Dh500 to 5,000. As utility bills are paid by a tenant, a refundable deposit of Dh1,000 to Dh2,000 normally has to be paid to the landlord for the use of water, electricity and gas. Some premises also require the payment of a 10 percent municipal tax. (Sharjah has a 5 percent municipal tax.)

Tenancy contracts normally last for a year, with Sharjah an exception, with three years being standard. Within that time, landlords cannot increase the rent.

Landlords normally have to handle the annual maintenance of their property, and they are not permitted to evict a tenant without just cause.

However, what is considered just cause in the UAE and Ireland differs, and as with all areas of life in the Emirates, there are cultural considerations to be aware of. For instance, if a group of people wants to house-share, they must all be of the same gender. Also, it is illegal for couples to live together unless they are married. Overseas unmarried couples sometimes live together and let people assume that they are married, but if the deceit is discovered, it could result in eviction, or at the least trouble with neighbours and the landlord. Bear in mind too that you can only sponsor a partner on your work visa if you are married.

## Property market

Until 2002, non-UAE citizens could not buy property on a freehold basis. Following a decree permitting overseas workers to buy freehold property in certain areas, a surge of demand sent prices booming. The surge has abated in the past year or two, with property prices steadying.

If you are buying, in all likelihood the property will be no more than ten years old. But despite the rush of developments, construction standards are good.

The type of property ranges from ground-floor villas to futuristic apartment buildings rising hundreds of metres above ground. If you are buying off-plan, personal luxuries, such as indoor swimming pools, can be included at cost.

Estate agents, both in the UAE and in Ireland, have plenty of Gulf state properties on their books.

## How to buy

Non-Emirates residents can arrange finance through local banks, which offer loan packages for up to fifteen-year periods.

## Property taxes

Owning a new property in the UAE will generally require the owner to contribute an annual service charge, which will vary according to the level of amenities provided.

# Utilities

There is usually a monopoly in each Emirate: Abu Dhabi Water and Electricity Company is the provider of power and water in the Emirate of Abu Dhabi, and Dubai Electricity and Water Authority provide electricity and water for the Emirate of Dubai.

# Education

Education is compulsory in the UAE for all children aged five and above, and state education is provided for UAE nationals up to the age of eighteen. There are also a number of local private schools. While there are a few universities in the UAE, the higher-education sector is limited.

The children of overseas workers living in the UAE generally attend one of the many international schools, which are all private and fee-paying. To apply for entry to one of the international schools, you will be required to show details of your child's academic record, and they may be required to sit an entrance test.

There is extremely wide variation in the fees for an international-school education, from around Dh 3,000 to 40,000 per year.

Note that a child cannot be transferred from one school to another once the academic year has begun, unless special permission is obtained from the Ministry of Education. Most English-speaking schools start their school year in September. If you plan to send your child to one of these schools, they will not be allowed to start school between 1 May and the end of the school year in June, but will have to wait until the beginning of the new school year. All schools are closed in July and August.

Normal school hours are from 8 AM to 1.30 PM, with some schools also providing afternoon sessions, for boys only, from noon to 5.30 PM.

## Driving

Holders of valid Irish driving licences can obtain a UAE licence without having to re-sit a test. As soon as your residency visa is completed, it is illegal for you to drive in the UAE on anything other than a valid UAE licence. You will also need to pass an eye test, which is available from most opticians.

# 14

# Destination Hong Kong

The economy of Hong Kong, the financial centre of East Asia, continues to function well side by side with China, and it has seen steady growth in recent years.

## Immigration

There are two main ways to get a work visa for Hong Kong: employer-sponsored, where you need a job before moving, and highly skilled independent, which is not conditional on a job offer.

The employer-sponsored option is more likely to bring success. Once you have obtained a job offer, your company will work with you in applying for a Hong Kong visa. Most applications are accepted.

There are some basic guidelines to immigration, and if one or more of these is not met, your application may be refused:

Applicants need to have a graduate degree or considerable technical experience in a certain area.

The applicant should also have relevant experience in the position they are applying for.

The individual will contribute to the local economy.

The company needs to prove that the position cannot be filled by a local person and/or that the applicant has a skill which is in short supply in the city.

The applicant has no criminal record.

The visa allows for a spouse and dependent children under eighteen to live in Hong Kong too.

Highly skilled applicants or wealthy investors can apply for residency in Hong Kong independent of a job offer. Points tests for skilled applicants and an economic contribution by investors were recently introduced by the Immigration Department of Hong Kong.

The points-test application is a quota-based 'skilled immigrants' program, whereby the applicant does not need a job offer in advance of entering Hong Kong. Two sets of points systems are used to evaluate applicants. These are the Achievement Based Points Test and the General Points Test.

Full details of all visas are available at *www.immd-.gov.hk*, the homepage of the Immigration Department of the Hong Kong Special Administrative Region.

The Region has an identity card system, and it is very important that, upon arrival, you register with the Immigration Department for a Hong Kong identity card. It is a statutory requirement for everyone aged eleven or over to carry the card at all times.

## Health care and social security

The standard of health care in Hong Kong is on a par with that of most European countries. Language should not be a great difficulty because many Hong Kong doctors are trained in the West. If you prefer, you should be able to find an American or English doctor, but they are likely to charge up to twice as much as a local Hong Kong doctor.

Hong Kong has some of the highest medical costs in the world, and so health insurance coverage is a must. Many insurance companies there are responding to the number of emigrants seeking policies by having professional advisors providing free quotations and detailed advice on health insurance needs in the region. Emigrants should carefully check job packages offered in Hong Kong, since health plans vary tremendously in terms of costs, coverage, and restrictions relating to doctors and treatments.

The Comprehensive Social Security Assistance (CSSA) Scheme and the Social Security Allowance (SSA) Scheme form the mainstay of Hong Kong's social security system. However, Hong Kong's social service benefits are only available to those who have been Hong Kong residents for at least seven years and have resided there continuously for at least one year immediately prior to the date of application.

# Taxation

Taxes are very low in Hong Kong, making it an attractive centre for international finance and banking. Income tax (or salary tax, as it is known) is set at 2 percent for those earning less than HK$35,000 a year, 8 percent for those earning HK$35,000 to HK$70,000, 14 percent for HK$70,000 to HK$105,000, and 20 percent for those earning more than HK$105,000.

At present, there is no sales tax, no capital gains tax, and no VAT.

# Employment

Unless you speak Cantonese fluently, you'll find there are only a limited number of professions and jobs open to English-speakers. These opportunities are primarily in banking and finance, teaching, media and hospitality.

It can be tough to find work in Hong Kong, as many overseas workers are there because they have been transferred by their company. Make as many inroads as you can before you arrive, using Irish-based and international employment agencies and recruitment specialists.

# Banking and finance

There are plenty of banks to choose from, as Hong Kong is the financial centre of East Asia and features one of the highest concentrations of banking institutions in the world. The region maintains a tier system of deposit-taking institutions, licensed banks, restricted-licence banks and deposit-taking companies. They are collectively known as authorised institutions by the Hong Kong Monetary Authority, which is responsible for regulations.

Hong Kong licensed banks may operate both current and savings accounts, and accept deposits of any size and maturity from the public. Services offered include credit cards and cheques.

# Accommodation

### Renting

Landlords are notoriously demanding in Hong Kong and rental prices are consistently high. You'll generally be expected to part with two months' rent as a security deposit and to hand over at least half a month's rent to the estate agent who finds your flat. (In Hong Kong, it is fairly common for a landlord to let his or her property through an estate agent.) You should also be prepared for high-rise, small-space living, as living space is at a premium.

## Property market and how to buy

A good place to find reliable information is the Hong Kong branches of international banks, such as the HSBC bank (which has a UK high-street presence). The websites of such banks have property listings on their websites.

As with lettings, estate agents are usually involved with managing the sale of properties. Most estate agents prefer that buyers and sellers enter into preliminary agreements, which become binding upon signing with payment of non-returnable deposits. You should take legal advice before signing the offer letter.

Most estate agents charge commission to both seller and buyer if they are acting for both parties; the figure is normally 1 percent for each party. However, this is negotiable.

Solicitors are used throughout most stages of the conveyancing transaction in Hong Kong. They are responsible for the sale and purchase agreement which is drafted by the seller's solicitor and approved by the buyer's solicitor.

You may have difficulty arranging a local mortgage. Prices are consistently very high due to the fact that there is very little property on the open market. Nearly half of Hong Kong's residents live in government housing, occupying spaces which may have entered the commercial property market at some stage.

Mortgages generally cover only 70 percent of the property price, with the balance to be raised from elsewhere.

The Hong Kong system of property transactions is based on the UK version (due to past British rule), with costs including:

A deposit of 5 percent payable on agreement in principle, and another 5 percent two weeks later

Broker fees of between 0.5 and 1 percent of the price

Solicitors' fees, generally in the region of HK$6,000

Stamp duty, anything between 0.75 and 3.75 percent of the purchase price.

# Utilities

Whether renting or buying, in general your estate agent will help you organise all your connections as part of the service.

You are usually asked for a deposit of two months' electricity charges. In some cases, this has already been paid for by the landlord, and you may simply take over paying the monthly bills. The electricity supply in Hong Kong is rated 200–220 volts. Plugs can be either square or round pin. Many older apartments have a mixture of both, so you may have to buy plug adapters.

China Light and Power generates and distributes electricity to around 80 percent of the households in Hong Kong: *www.clpgroup.com*.

The Hong Kong Electric Company supplies electricity to Hong Kong and Lamma Island: *www.heh.com*. Towngas (*www.hkcg.com*) supplies gas to 1.3 million households and businesses in Hong Kong. To open an account with Towngas, you'll need to pay a deposit. Older apartments, especially those in parts of the New Territories and apartments in the Outlying Islands, are not connected to the gas main. In this case, you will need to use bottled gas, which can be delivered.

Water bills are minimal in Hong Kong; the Water Supplies Department issues bills quarterly.

TELEVISION   Hong Kong has two free Chinese-language channels and two free English-language channels (Pearl and ATV World), for which you don't need to pay any fees. Pay TV operators and broadband providers can supply internet and a wide range of additional channels.

# Education

Hong Kong's education system is similar to the English system.

Schools in Hong Kong tend to have strict codes of discipline, and nearly all students in the territory wear a school uniform.

The immigrant community is well served for education through private and international schools. However, you should make your choice of school a priority, as there are invariably waiting lists for the best establishments.

While the international schools receive a grant from the Hong Kong government, parents face hefty tuition fees.

# Driving

Hong Kong's public transport system works well and is safer and cheaper than that in most international cities.

You can drive in Hong Kong on a foreign licence temporarily when you arrive, but if you're staying more than a year, you must get a Hong Kong licence in order to keep driving.

If you have an Irish licence, you can use it to apply for a Hong Kong licence without having to re-sit a test. As the traffic system is very similar to that used in the UK, traffic lights, road signs and marking will be very familiar.

# A Final Word

You should now be more assured about the process of living and working abroad. And even if you have a specific question that remains unanswered, you'll have an idea of where to find the necessary information. Hopefully, reading this book will have prompted some questions that you otherwise wouldn't have thought of.

And when it comes to emigrating, ignorance isn't bliss. Even getting routine paperwork – for instance, replacement college certificates if you have lost your originals – can be an interminable pain in the ass when you need them to apply for or qualify for a job and are eating into your savings in the meantime.

Indeed, bureaucracy, paperwork and red tape will prove to be some of the most frustrating aspects of the emigration process. This is one area where being as prepared as possible will save considerable heartache and annoyance later on.

But the potential rewards of emigrating are there for all to see, and should always be kept in mind, especially at difficult times during the move.

Will all your problems and difficulties in life simply disappear if you leave Ireland?

No.

Will emigrating provide new prospects, new friends,

new challenges, a new home, a new job, and maybe even a new you?

Yes.

Unquestionably, living and working abroad offers the tantalising prospect of a 'clean slate'.

Despite the bureaucratic hurdles – and all the other challenges outlined in the book – thousands of people make the move each year and don't regret it.

There is a world of possibilities beyond Ireland, and on your travels you're likely to meet those other Irish people who have enjoyed life-enriching experiences as a result of emigrating.

So if you also feel you're ready to begin a new chapter in the story of your life – go for it.